D1601080

BEYOND BUREAUCRACY

A blueprint and vision for government that works

Kenneth Johnston

BUSINESS ONE IRWIN
Homewood, Illinois 60430

© KENNETH JOHNSTON, 1993

This publication is designed to provide accurate and authoritative information in regard to the subject matter covered. It is sold with the understanding that neither the author nor the publisher is engaged in rendering legal, accounting, or other professional service. If legal advice or other expert assistance is required, the services of a competent professional person should be sought.

From a Declaration of Principles jointly adopted by a Committee of the American Bar Association and a Committee of Publishers.

Editor-in-chief: Jeffrey A. Krames
Project editor: Jane Lightell
Production manager: Mary Jo Parke
Designer: Andrea Jensen
Printer: Book Press, Inc.

Library of Congress Cataloging-in-Publication Data

Johnston, Kenneth B.
  Beyond bureaucracy : a blueprint and vision for government that works / Kenneth B. Johnston.
      p.   cm.
  Includes bibliographical references (p.   ).
  ISBN 1–55623–990–4
  1. Organizational change. 2. Organizational effectiveness.
  3. Bureaucracy. 4. Public administration. I. Title.
  JF 1525.073J64   1993
  350—dc20   92–41913

Printed in the United States of America

1 2 3 4 5 6 7 8 9 0 BP 9 8 7 6 5 4 3 2

This book is warmly dedicated to members of the Administration, Congressional Representatives, Senators, Cabinet Secretaries, and other heads of governmental agencies at the federal, state and municipal levels. In addition, this book is dedicated to the millions of government workers who spend whole careers working in agencies immobilized and suffocated by bureaucracy. You deserve better! I hope this book will help you find a better way.

Acknowledgments

This book exists because Kathy Cook Farzanegan, Peg Anthony, Chuck Lalonde, Barry Bauer, Susan Davis, and virtually the entire Government team from Kaset International urged me to write it.

Many examples of debureaucratizing efforts by governmental agencies were contributed by the account managers, trainers, and consultants from Kaset International. Specifically, I thank Beth Potter, Bill Crump, Brenda Cudworth, Bruce Hammond, Carly Holliday, Cindi Grande, Claude Speed, Gary Richardson, Donna Jensen, Janet Hoch, Karen Loeffler, Kellylynn Pipkin, Linda Burke, Marie Beaugrand, Mario Macaluso, Michael Hajaistron, Penny Thomas-Kezar, Sarah Fyvolent, Sean Crosbie, and Sharon Daniels.

The manuscript was greatly improved, polished, and expanded by the renowned author Jeff Davidson, who added his own passion and conviction honed by years of working for the federal government.

The book itself was produced from the manuscript by the extensive work of Shannon Johnston, Andrea Jensen, Jeffrey Krames, Amy Smith, and the support of Sarah Kruse.

The cartoons were created by Don Baumgart, who besides being a cartoon genius, is a retired high school principal and well acquainted with bureaucracy as it exists in public education.

I am indebted to my father and mother, Ken and Edythe Johnston, who taught me to care about government and urged me to do what I could to contribute to government that works.

I want to thank Dave Erdman for doing my work so I could take the time to write this book.

Finally, I wish to thank my friend Dick Woltmann, Director, Bay Area Legal Services, for showing me that it is possible to create a world-class public-sector organization by making it customer focused.

Table of Contents

Introduction

I wrote *Beyond Bureaucracy* in response to those who read my book **Busting Bureaucracy** (written primarily for the private sector), and asked me or my company, Kaset International, how the same ideas could be used to improve federal, state, and local government. Several members of Congress, for example, asked us to help them understand why the citizens in their states are so angry, disgusted, and/or cynical about government in general and Congress in particular.

Several federal agencies requested our help in redesigning their agencies to make them "customer focused," to gain, or regain, public support. In my home state of Florida, I personally was asked to write a "vision" to help restructure public education throughout the state. (Parts of this are included herein as Chapter Twelve.)

Over the years I have observed that almost universally, people—citizens—like the *idea* of government. They agree that certain functions, such as building and maintaining the infrastructure or national defense, can only be executed by government. However, problems surface when you move from the *concept* of government and how it is supposed to operate, to the *reality* of our government and how it does work.

As a general observation, citizens today don't like the government they have and don't think that government works well. They don't like the way that federal government works or the way state government works, and they're not keen on local government either.

People I've encountered from all walks of life do not think government produces good results, operates efficiently, or yields good value for the tax dollar. They are almost uniformly negative about "bureaucrats," and they hate "bureaucracy." Not ironically, many people *in government* feel the same way.

Citizens' attitudes toward government today range from rage to apathy. They do not hold their government in respect, nor speak proudly about the way government serves the people. Perhaps most important, citizens don't like the way they are treated by government employees.

Don't be confused by ample signs of patriotism or low emigration figures here in the United States. Few of our citizens think our system is worse than socialism, monarchy, or dictatorships. Only a few people are willing to contribute more in taxes, because most are convinced that the government wastes much of the money that it gets now. This is a crucial issue.

Citizens *would be untroubled with paying more taxes* if they felt assured that government expenditures were well spent. A dramatic example of this issue can be seen in public education. Citizens want better schools and better education, but I believe that they vote against more taxes for education because they are convinced they would get "more of the same" with higher costs.

Although they often seem to like the few politicians that they can identify by name, in increasing numbers citizens dislike and distrust politicians as a group. This dislike has been evidenced by recent furor over the attempted congressional pay raise, the movement to limit congressional terms, financial reform efforts aimed at limiting political contributions, open records reform efforts, and the recent, "Throw the Hypocritical Rascals Out" movement. At the state level, we've witnessed massive public demonstrations against incumbent governors, particularly in Connecticut, Florida, and Massachusetts.

During economic downturns, it is easy to blame government for a variety of ills; that fact can explain some of the public dissatisfaction. I believe, however, that the growing discontent with government goes deeper than just a weak or fluctuating economy. From an historic perspective it is too early to be certain, but the emergence of deep discontent may be because we "won" the war against communism.

In the absence of competing systems of government against which to compare our system of government, Americans are beginning to compare our system against something different—their expectations and hopes for what government could be.

Some people believe that the discontent is related to a rising tide of consumer expectations in dealing with the private sector, which has spilled over into the public sector. Others feel that the high-minded cohort of 74,000,000 baby-boomers is now in position to make demands on government delivery systems.

Regardless of its origin, the discontent is profound, widespread, and still growing. Its derivation is not nearly as important as the recognition that it is not likely to pass soon. If my guess is correct, we can expect increasing amounts of citizen dissatisfaction throughout the 1990s. Government *will have to change*, that is certain. Will the change, however, lead us toward a better society or toward something else?

This book is for you if you want to make things better around you, even if it is just your department representing only a small part of the government agency where you work. While achieving a major shift in organizing form, especially away from the bureaucratic organizing form, requires the long-term commitment of top agency officials, there are things you can do, as Theodore Roosevelt once said, "with what you have, where you are."

Chapter One

Why citizens don't like government

5

Americans are beginning to compare our system of government against their expectations and hopes for what government "could" or "should" achieve.

This book is intended for people who work in bureaucratic agencies at all levels of federal, state, or local government. It is designed to be circulated among managers to stimulate dialogue, build commitment, and facilitate decisions regarding possible changes to the agency. It is also designed to be given to people not in managerial positions, so they might participate in the decision to change, and so they will understand any "change effort" that top agency officials decide to undertake.

The goal of the book is to help you learn the following:

1. Your agency is organized using what is called the "bureaucratic form."

2. All agencies suffer the same suffocating and immobilizing symptoms that people call "bureaucracy."

3. Most employees blame their agency's "bureaucracy" on top officials. They assume that management must want it, or it wouldn't be tolerated.

4. Top officials don't want or like "bureaucracy" any more than the rest of the agency's employees. The detestable effects of bureaucracy victimize everyone, regardless of level.

5. The root cause of "bureaucracy" is the organizing model, the "bureaucratic form." Yet, the bureaucratic form is so pervasive that its destructive nature is seldom questioned.

6. If you were starting a new agency today, you could avoid "bureaucracy" by using a new organizing model called the "mission-driven" model, which we'll explore within.

7. Existing bureaucratic agencies can reduce the amount of "bureaucracy" by changing one or more of the basic organizing principles, either temporarily or permanently.

Let's see what can be done to create a government that works.

All too familiar

At our company, when we ask people in different occupations from different parts of the country why they aren't satisfied with government, the reasons they give sound extremely familiar to us—I'll explain momentarily.

- They think that government agencies are run to serve their own interests, rather than for serving the citizens.

- They have no direct personal experience of improved service or responsiveness and haven't seen tangible evidence elsewhere.

- They think that government agencies are "bureaucratic," exhibiting a wide range of symptoms: they see government agencies as being inflexible, unresponsive, disorganized, error-prone, and top-heavy with layers of excess management while being too lean at the bottom to adequately meet constituent needs.

- They are pessimistic that the various federal agencies will succeed in handling the critical issues entrusted to them.

They don't think that government, for example, can solve the drug problem. They don't believe that the Department of Commerce can stimulate commerce. They don't think that the Department of Education has improved education or will do so in the foreseeable future. They don't think that the Justice Department will reduce crime. They don't think that the Department of Labor will help working people, and on and on. The pessimism is the same or worse with government at the state level and local level.

Some believe that agencies focus on the wrong issues, or on the right issues but in the wrong manner. Others feel that the problems have grown too big and are now unmanageable. Still others believe that government has no real sensitivity to the needs of its citizens. The federal government, commonly referred to as "Washington" is seen as out of touch with the rest of the country, unable to understand concerns beyond the Capital Beltway, and relentlessly engaged in self-perpetuation.

People dealing with specific agencies of government, whether federal, state, or local, report feeling "trapped" or "helpless" because the agency is fundamentally a monopoly.

Feeling trapped or helpless

A woman from Kansas City calls a federal agency in Washington one afternoon only to be told, matter-of-factly, that it's 4:45 p.m. on the east coast and she'll have to call back tomorrow between 8:30 a.m. and 4:30 p.m. EST.

The next day, she calls back as instructed and before she's had a chance to fully explain who she'd like to reach, a harried switchboard operator connects her with the wrong office. A well-meaning but uninformed staff person forwards her to call to yet another wrong office, at which time she is given a completely different number and told to call there.

She dials, but the number is incessantly busy. After many attempts, hours later, she gets through. At last, she's got the right office, but the person who could best help her is unavailable at this time. She is asked to call back in two hours. Each of her calls adds to her long distance phone bill, at the premier weekday rate. She'd write instead of call, but from past efforts she knows that it would take weeks if not months to get a reply, and then perhaps not even a useful reply.

When she finally gets to the right person, she politely is given a set of instructions. These instructions include filling out a form, which happens to be out of stock at the moment.

Multiply her experience by millions of other citizens' attempts to make direct contact with government, at any level, and you have the portrait of a colossal, continuing nightmare. How can you fight the local water commission, for example, when they are the only source of regularly running water to your home?

Citizens who tell us about being dissatisfied with an agency, often describe the agency's response as arrogant and dictatorial, with agency representatives acting more like hostage-takers than public servants.

Why, pray tell, are all of these responses familiar to us at Kaset? They are identical to responses we have been gathering for years from customers of electric utilities, gas companies, telephone companies, and recently, cable companies. All of these organizations, like government, are monopolistic bureaucracies.

Some important distinctions

Common use of the term *bureaucracy* can be confusing because the word has many interpretations. *Bureaucracy* has at least three different meanings:

1. Civil service employees of the U.S. government are commonly referred to as "the bureaucracy," as in the sentence: "The threat of Gramm-Rudman-Hollings cuts has the bureaucracy in Washington deeply concerned."

2. "Bureaucracy" is the name of the organizing form or model used by sociologists and organizational design specialists.

3. "Bureaucracy" is used informally to describe the negative by-products of using the organizing form, as in the sentence: "There is too much bureaucracy where I work." This informal usage is synonymous with the "red tape," or "inflexibility" that frustrate people who deal with, or who work for organizations they perceive as "bureaucratic."

To keep the distinctions clear, in this book:

When I refer to people—career government employees—I'll say "the bureaucracy," or "bureaucrats."

When I refer to the organizational form, despite the wordiness, I'll link the words *form* or *model* with the word *bureaucratic* or *bureaucracy*.

When I refer to the negative by-products, "nonsense," or "sludge," that you and I mean when we talk about having "too much bureaucracy," I'll use the terms *bureaucracy* or *bureaucratic* without the article "the," without the plural *bureaucrats*, and without the linking words *form or model.*

Illustration:

The **bureaucrats** in local government appear very **bureaucratic** to the public because they are organized based on the **bureaucracy** organizing model.

Why is government the way it is?

When we ask people why government is unresponsive, they blame politicians, bureaucrats, and our system of government itself. They often describe politicians, and political appointees as well, as being self-serving, untrustworthy people who are primarily interested in keeping their offices and getting what they can for themselves.

- They cite politicians' frequent promises to change government, but when the promises are not kept, people often assume that politicians don't want to make changes. They also believe that politicians will bend to the pressures of special interests, rather than doing "what's right."

- They describe bureaucrats as being overstaffed, overpaid, lazy, greedy, underworked, insolent, indifferent, and more interested in following in-focused or self-serving procedures than serving the public.

- They blame our system of government, including one or both of the major parties, and the lack of choices at the polls.

(A small number of the people we talked to blame ineffective government on those who choose not to vote; others regard voting itself as futile and sympathize with non-voters.)

I find it especially noteworthy that government employees, politicians, and appointees possess many of these same attitudes and opinions about government. As one of many in my organization who have spent thousands of professional staff hours in focus groups and in one-on-one conversations with government employees, we've found that within government, groups tend to blame other groups, rather than their own group, and right now blaming others is at epidemic proportions.

People inside government are more aware than citizens are of waste, mediocrity, and bureaucracy. There seems to be a growing feeling of hopelessness about the situation, with few good answers. The old solutions apparently didn't work, and new ones don't seem that attractive.

Good people who were attracted to government service in hopes of making a difference get discouraged and leave. Or they get discouraged and stay. In any case, the majority of people in government to whom we've spoken, report that they frequently feel negative, pessimistic, and cynical about their agency or about government in general. Many feel that they are "spinning their wheels," merely putting in their time and drawing a paycheck with attractive government benefits.

Again, we are familiar with these attitudes and responses, because we also find them, to a lesser degree, in the ranks of employees within other monopolistic bureaucracies.

Simply put, the bureaucratic form of organizing is at the root of citizen dissatisfaction with government just as it is at the root of customer dissatisfaction with public services.

A thorn by any other name

Because the roots of citizen dissatisfaction and customer dissatisfaction are the same, for ease of wording and to shift your focus about how government can work, I shall employ the term *customer dissatisfaction* for the balance of the book to refer to all manner of discontent with government on the part of those whom government is intended to serve. I'll use *customer satisfaction* to refer to the opposite situation, and I shall call people whom government is intended to serve *customers*.

Using the terms *customer*, *customer satisfaction* and *customer dissatisfaction* in this manner serves as constant reminder that citizens—taxpayers, voters, dependents, all manner of Americans—are the *customers of government*. Government exists to serve the collective interests of the people, and nothing more.

The rise of bureaucracy

In the 1930's, Max Weber, a German sociologist, described bureaucracy as the ideal organizing model for governmental agencies. Although Weber's views have been largely discredited since then, and the failures of bureaucracy amply demonstrated, there has been little serious examination of better ways to organize governmental agencies. It is frightening that the bureaucratic organizing form has flourished for so long and has remained relatively unchallenged.

In may ways, Weber did for bureaucracy what Lenin did for communism—glorified it to the hilt and positioned it as a social cure-all. Like Lenin, Weber also failed to consider the downstream damage such a concept would have on a society's economic and social structures.

I believe that bureaucracy was a primary factor in the demise of communism. I believe that bureaucracy has socialism in a death grip. If we don't take action, I believe that bureaucracy will immobilize and suffocate our government as well.

Because of the enormous citizen pressure, there are many examples of agencies *attempting* to change, such as adopting total quality management (TQM) principles or becoming customer focused.

We have not found evidence of any agency, however, actually challenging the basic model upon which it is organized—the bureaucratic form of government. This leads to the conclusion that agencies are attacking the *symptoms* of bureaucracy, rather than the "root cause."

Under pressure of global competition, many private sector firms—General Electric and Ford Motor Company, for example—have already replaced the bureaucratic organizing form with new organizing paradigms. Virtually all of the agencies of government would improve their productivity, customer satisfaction, and employee satisfaction by replacing the bureaucracy model with either a different organizing form, or a modified form of bureaucracy that works more efficiently.

Government works poorly, particularly when compared with our expectations and hopes. The problem isn't the politicians, appointees, or government workers. The problem is that *our government is based on the bureaucratic organizing form—and thus functions as a bureaucracy*. Government is staffed by good people who could live up to the hopes and expectations of the citizenry if they were organized using a more effective organizing form.

In the balance of this book I will:

- illuminate the true nature of the bureaucratic form of government so that each of us, at all levels, can work to break free of its grip, and

- offer several more effective models for organizing governmental agencies.

Chapter Two

What makes an agency seem bureaucratic?

Agencies established on the bureaucratic form exhibit many objectionable characteristics that their customers and employees describe as being bureaucratic.

Citizens who report being dissatisfied with governmental agencies, or businesses for that matter, often refer to them as being *bureaucratic*, especially if an organization:

- Seems so focused on meeting only the organization's needs, that it does not appear concerned with the customer's needs.

- Has rigid policies and procedures, which customers call "red tape," and seems inflexible and unresponsive to customer's needs.

- Seems intent with giving customers "equal treatment" and seems unaware that equal treatment produces "unequal satisfaction," or even widespread *dissatisfaction*.

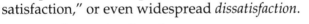

- Appears "uncaring," and treats customers more like "numbers" than individuals. Makes getting an exception to a rule difficult or impossible.

- Seldom innovates, and seems reluctant to change as times change or events dictate. When change does occur it is seen as long overdue, seldom comprehensive, and with limited long-term effectiveness.

- Offers products and services of inferior quality compared with non-bureaucratic organizations.

- Is difficult to reach during the work day, and busy periods may virtually be unreachable.

- Seems arrogant or humorless.

- Is unwilling to admit mistakes, and
  attempts to shift blame for their
  own mistakes onto
  the customer,
  or onto
  other
  groups
  within the
  bureaucracy.

Other characteristics reported include employees who are not positive about the agency, who give the impression that they aren't happy to be working there, and who are less than enthusiastic about the organization's products or services.

Within the agencies themselves, employees witness or are party to a host of nonproductive, nonsupportive behaviors. Employees speak of an organization as being bureaucratic when:

- Each department has its own agenda, and departments won't cooperate to help other departments get the job done.

- People in their own department spend much of their time protecting the department's "turf," or their own derrieres.

- People in *other* departments spend so much time protecting their "turf" that they don't have time to achieve their unit's mission.

- Employees are treated as though they can't be trusted or as if they don't have good judgment. They are treated as if they won't work hard unless pushed.

- There is political in-fighting, with executives seemingly striving for personal power rather than achievement of a mission.
- This work environment includes large amounts of unhealthy stress.
- Promotions are made more on the basis of politics than effectiveness on the job.
- Top officials are perilously ill-informed and insulated.

Employees feel they are victims of bureaucracy when their agency tends to grow top-heavy in terms of management and functional staff, while the operating levels of the agency are starved for staff and become bottom-lean.

Top-heavy and bottom-lean

All the evidence suggests that the bureaucratic form leads government agencies to become top-heavy and bottom-lean. The hierarchical design of the bureaucracy results in the administrative and management segment of the agency growing steadily over time, regardless of what happens to the operating segment (the lower ranks) of the agency. When a budget squeeze comes, agencies look first to save money by cutting services at "the bottom" of the agency.

Governmental agencies cut services at the bottom of the agency for two reasons. First, it's the people near the top of the agency who decide who gets cut. Second, if the agency does provide a needed service, the taxpayers will feel "the pinch" faster by cuts near the bottom of the agency, and may show greater responsiveness to agency appeals for more money.

In the autumn of 1990, the U.S. Congress, the President, and his administration were racing to agree on a deficit reduction plan before the Gramm-Rudman-Hollings Act would force automatic, across-the-board cuts. On a Tuesday, the federal government would be forced to make huge cuts unless Congress and the President agreed on a new budget over a long holiday weekend.

> *The agency that governs public lands and parks closed national parks and monuments to tourists on Saturday of the long weekend presumably to disappoint and frustrate citizens as visibly and obviously as possible as a way of focusing attention on what the people would lose if government budgets were cut.*
>
> *A major city ordered percentage cuts, as another example, across the board in all agencies. In every department, the agencies made the bulk of their cuts in the lower levels of the agency. Particularly noticeable were the fire department and the police department, where the cuts were made in front-line people. The "top heavy" ranks were scarcely touched. The agency's self interests were best served by reducing services, thus putting the maximum possible imposition on the citizens— in hopes that the citizens would demand that their particular budgets be restored.*

Taxpayers, legislators, and the media will not succeed in cutting waste and bloat in government as long as cuts are administered more heavily on the lower ranks of governmental agencies than on the upper ranks.

What else is known about bureaucratic agencies

Employees in bureaucratic agencies report other attributes that they describe as "bureaucracy."

- Internal communications to employees are distorted to reflect what the agency would like to be.

- Data is used selectively, or distorted to make performance look better than it actually is. Worse, quantitative measurements are favored over qualitative measurements, so the concentration is on quantities of output with less and less concern for quality of output.

- Responsibility for mistakes and failure tends to be denied, and where possible, blame is shifted to others—a daily ritual in Congress, the Administration, and most agencies.

- Decisions are made by larger and larger groups, so no one can be held accountable. Or, decisions are made at higher and higher levels with many layers of approvals required.

- Decisions are made based on the perceived desires of superiors, rather than concern for mission achievement.

Employees say that personal issues and human needs are discounted or ignored. These frustrated employees find that agency policies, practices, and procedures grow endlessly and become more and more rigid.

Finally, and perhaps most discouraging, employees and top agency officials with the best of intentions feel *overwhelmed* at the difficulty of changing the way their agency or unit works. Appointees in particular come with high hopes and boundless ambitions, especially when they first come on board. Many see themselves as the ones who will make a difference.

In less than a year, and sometimes in matter of months or weeks, their hopes may become muted by the cloud of resignation that looms in every corridor. *Almost no one gets out with their ambitions intact.* At first, newcomers to government settle for what seems to be an effective compromise with themselves, e.g., "Maybe I can't accomplish it all, but I can probably tackle A, B, and C." Soon enough, personal survival becomes the primary issue.

In short, bureaucracy as seen by customers and employees, top officials, appointees, and career veterans, is an array of negative forces, attitudes, or actions that are damaging to customer and employee satisfaction, and to an agency's effectiveness. It weakens employee morale and commitment. It divides people and departments within the agency, and misdirects their energy into conflict with each other instead of toward the mission of the agency.

Why, then, has a form of organization that produces such abominable by-products lasted so long? Let's take a look.

Chapter Three

What did the bureaucratic model promise?

The undesirable attributes of bureaucracy are not the fault of the people in the organization. They occur any time an entity is organized on the bureaucratic form.

The bureaucratic form of government is so common today that most people accept it as the norm, if not the *only* way of organization. They have endured it because it promises major benefits. In reality, the bureaucratic form evolved in a different era, and promised to solve different problems than those that exist today.

Weber's model of bureaucracy was comprised of six major principles or components, each of which was designed to provide certain advantages.

1. A formal hierarchical structure

In the bureaucratic form of government, each level controls the level below and is controlled by the level above. Decision authority is based on organizational level. A formal hierarchy is the basis of central planning, decision making, and control. Theoretically, the top official would have control over the entire agency, and the outside world would know who to hold responsible. "The captain of the ship is responsible for whatever happens on or to the ship."

In Max Weber's day, when bureaucracy in the U.S. was beginning to flower, the world of business and government was drastically different than it is today. Prior to industrialization, agencies were smaller and management skills usually were required only at the very top. In an agency where uppermost officials were educated, and staff members less so—it appeared essential to focus on control.

Where the hierarchy breaks down

The hierarchical design of the bureaucracy model leads to the kind of central planning that, almost single-handedly, has been the downfall of state socialism and communism around the world. Central planning may be necessary in the military and perhaps in a few other select agencies of government. For most other agencies of government, however, central planning and control doom their chances for success from the outset.

As more layers are added to an agency, and more controls added, the time in which decisions can be reached and action taken even on the smallest of issues is prolonged. Staff come to be dependent on answers from above, while those at higher levels are removed from the challenges faced by rank and file staff and from the needs of customers.

2. Management by rules

Controlling by rules allows decisions made at high levels to be executed consistently by all lower levels, and hence management by rules promises control and consistency. If the entire agency was managed by rules, then top officials could ensure that the agency would be controlled by their decisions, and that no arbitrary or inconsistent judgment could be introduced. The head of the agency could decide how things would be done—and forever after they would be done that way.

Consistency was appealing because the world of our forefathers was marked by inconsistency. People were discriminated against because of class, education, race, religion, or creed. Some enjoyed advantages because of birth, education, or social status. In a era when people were apt to be dealt dissimilarly from each other, consistency was regarded as highly desirable.

Where management by rules breaks down

Governmental agencies typically are formed by legislators, through legislation, and thus are born through laws, the toughest form of rules. As a consequence, agencies typically don't have as much choice about turning "rules" into "guidelines" that can be put aside when they interfere with the agency's mission. This means that most government agencies feel forced to follow their rules even though the people involved may be fully aware that the rules do not result in achieving the agency's mission.

The control promised by management by rules turns out to be illusory. One of the first lessons that a newly appointed Cabinet level Secretary learns is that the "control" you had hoped for is quite limited. As Secretary, you learn that rules can work when you want to stop something.

In the well-formed bureaucracy, however, it is more difficult to "start" things, or make good things happen. As a result, the bureaucratic model allows top officials to "not do" certain kinds of things, but isn't as helpful in getting the agency to "do" things. At the federal level, Secretaries who want to make their agencies "customer focused," or employ "total quality management" find either choice impossible to achieve unless they let go of the bureaucratic model and begin using principles from other organizing models. Otherwise, no amount of management by rules give the Secretary or senior officials enough "control" to enable their agency to offer high quality service or achieve customer satisfaction.

Challenging situations need not be faced by the bureaucrat who consults a rule book that readily provides answers, if not solutions.

When applied across the board to all manner of concerns, rules tend to support bureaucratic procedure while serving only the needs of those customers who are lucky enough to have the rules match their needs, or those who have the resources to navigate within the narrow confines of the rules.

Consider the widow whose bread-winning spouse dies, days before qualifying for maximum benefits under a given retirement scenario.

Under management by rules, the spouse will have to settle for partial payment for the rest of her life.

Every day, thousands of customers who deal with government learn that through no fault of their own, they are a day late, or early, or a dollar short, or a dollar too much, to qualify for benefits that will affect the quality of the rest of their lives.

Management by rules can become absurd in situations such as the State Department of Revenue where a taxpayer who owes a few cents receives one computer-generated letter after another.

3. Organization by functional specialty

Agencies are assigned specific tasks or formed to work on specific issues. People within the agencies are organized into units based on the type of work they do, or skills they have.

Early on, specialization of sub-units promised accountability, control, and expertise. If specialists were in charge of each function of the agency, then top officials could be certain that an educated or trained person was responsible for that function. Moreover they could be fairly confident that the people handling that function were expert in that function. Both of these benefits promised more control and greater effectiveness.

In the 1800s, people were often given responsibility for managing on the basis of their wealth, class, or family—not necessarily because they were trained or skilled. Thus, having specialists seemed like a big improvement over having managers who were selected through favoritism.

Where organization by functional specialty breaks down

The responsibility and accountability that are promised by organizing according to functional specialty are easily and often subverted. Anyone employed by a bureaucracy for more than a couple of weeks quickly learns the many different ways to avoid responsibility and accountability. The strategies range from not doing anything, to taking no risks, to stifling innovation, or to getting many additional signatures.

Fully-formed bureaucracies can even penalize people for *taking* responsibility and being accountable. Consider the stigma attached to becoming a "whistleblower." The very name suggests that the reporting party is guilty of causing more disturbance than the transgression he or she has brought to light. At the Nurenberg trials following World War II, Nazi underlings who claimed to be only "following orders" were given little sympathy in their sentences. Yet, in many government bureaucracies today, "following orders" is more strongly supported than initiative and mission achievement.

Organization by specialty quite often gets in the way of customer satisfaction. To get a new addition to my house built, I may need permits or inspection by a number of different city agencies. To move your aging mother to the proper long-term care facility in a cost-effective manner, you may need guidance that cuts across the lines of functional specialties. Any customer request to a government agency that requires the attention of more than one functional specialist is subject to inordinate delay, or worse, neglect.

4. An "up-focused" or "in-focused" mission

A mission defines what the agency is established to do, and how it intends to measure itself. If the success of the agency depends on satisfying the customer, then the mission needs to be focused on customer satisfaction.

In government as presently structured, an agency's underlying mission almost always is to serve the legislature, Congress, or body that empowered it. That makes virtually every government agency "up-focused."

The idea seemed sound, because it promised that an agency of government would not end up serving the people who were in the agency, nor would it end up serving people outside of the agency. Instead, it would theoretically serve the government—hence, all the people.

The EPA, for example, will state that its mission is to clean up the environment, and DOD will state that its mission is to protect against aggression. Because the bureaucracy model forces them to be up-focused, they might often be perceived as behaving as though their mission is to serve the appropriations committee that funds them.

"In-focused missions" are missions that aim at achieving some internal goal that will benefit the agency itself, rather than benefit its customers (for example, increased funding, or increased staffing). Agencies that have less governance from above find it tempting to alter their mission orientation to serve their own internal goals and thus become "in-focused." The FBI and the CIA have been cited by critics as examples here.

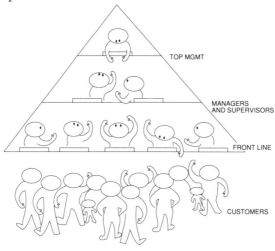

In-Focused Organization

As is painfully evident now, an "up-focused" mission or an "in-focused" mission keeps the agency from being customer focused. Customers know this and feel this. The great paradox is that customers, through taxes, pay to keep operational the legislature, Congress, or agency that empowered these in-focused or up-focused agencies.

5. Purposely impersonal

The idea behind this principle of the bureaucratic organizing form is to treat all employees and customers equally, and not be influenced by individual differences. Being impersonal theoretically promises objectivity, consistency, and equality. Weber held that if you wipe out the human elements of the transaction, and focus only on the "administrative" side, you could be sure that no customer was treated better or worse than another. If you treat everyone identically, as though they had no individual differences, then you could ensure consistency and fairness through equal treatment.

Equal treatment was highly valued as bureaucracies first emerged because many people felt they didn't get treated equally with those of wealth, power, or influence. Over the long decades, however, as agency employees execute their duties impersonally, two things tend to happen:

1. the execution of their duties actually becomes *less* purposeful
2. their ability and desire to respond to real human needs diminishes.

Where purposely impersonal falls short

While being impersonal promises, and largely delivers objectivity, equality of treatment, and consistency, the problem is that neither customers nor employees are satisfied by being equally treated. They actually want to be equally satisfied, which requires treating some people differently, which leads to Johnston's law:

Johnston's law:

If you treat everyone the same, what varies is satisfaction. To achieve equal satisfaction, you must vary treatment.

People don't want to be all treated the same. They want their differences to be respected. The bureaucratic form promises equal treatment for everybody and essentially says, "We want to be fair. We want to treat everybody alike. We want to treat everybody the way that we want to be treated, and we will expect everyone to live up to our expectations."

You can't remove the human element when dispensing services to human beings. Functionally competent health service organizations that don't understand this can't compete with those that do. Private-sector businesses that ignore the human element in serving customers fall by the wayside. Agencies that deal impartially with customers are accused of being uncaring, unkind, and unresponsive —in a word, bureaucratic. We've found that:

Once customers characterize an organization as bureaucratic, they also tend to believe that the organization *dispenses inferior services*.

Agency employees don't respond well either

Purposely impersonal treatment of agency employees works poorly when put into practice. A fixed set of benefits ensures variable satisfaction. A "cafeteria" approach to benefits, allowing each person to choose according to their individual situation and needs, offers a better chance of uniform satisfaction. A fixed set of work hours, or vacation times, or what have you, similarly ignores the human needs of agency employees.

6. Employment based on technical qualifications

Job security was little known in the early 20th Century, but was highly valued and highly prized, nevertheless. Employment based on technical qualifications promised equal opportunity, and protection from arbitrary dismissal promised job security to those who could pass a test and follow the rules.

Equal opportunity meant that a middle-class educated person had the same opportunity of entry into government as an upper-class or wealthy person. That equal opportunity was valued in an era when government tended to be dominated by those with money, power, or influence.

Where employment based on technical qualifications breaks down

Hiring based on technical qualifications without regard to individual differences or subjective issues, such as personality, aptitude, disposition for the job, or the ability to learn and grow, or to cooperate as part of a team, all too frequently leads to bad hiring decisions.

While mayor of New York, John Lindsay forced the city's public utilities to hire people who passed minimum technical qualifications for particular jobs. Many were lacking personality characteristics regarded as significant for successfully executing the various jobs. Although his intentions were good—segments of the workforce were underrepresented—the utilities began filling positions with individuals who, in many cases, did not have the work or customer skills to fit the job.

Some employees were placed as telephone operators for the utility, a position that requires being able to effectively handle irate callers. As author Dave Yoho notes in his book, How to Have a Good Year Every Year *(Berkley), without having the background and demeanor necessary to defuse potentially tense situations, these employees "were subjected to incredible stress" and many "eventually quit what was otherwise the best paying jobs that they had ever held."*

"Because someone else," Yoho says, "such as a boss, a manager, or a mayor, didn't place them in a set of conditions in which they could be

successful, many lost confidence in themselves which quite possibly impacted their future employment and entire career."

In addition, as a result of restricting their hiring to people who are only "technically qualified," many agencies do not have, and cannot generate, the necessary commitment among the rank and file to make "service quality" improvement the driving force in their agency.

What else does bureaucracy do to government?

The bureaucratic model also fragments government into specialized agencies concerned with their own special interests. They are not chartered to take a broad view, and sometimes are not even allowed to. They have to encourage citizens to be concerned with their cause or they will not get funded. A real problem for career government workers is that if they actually do solve their particular social problem, the need for the agency might disappear.

In some cases, the self-interest of the agency can gradually become *opposite* to the interest of the public. Witness the competing elements of government today that either *subsidize tobacco growers*, or seek to put the industry out of business.

One agency's charter says one thing, and 20 years of in-depth studies by the Office of the Surgeon General says another. A tobacco industry lobbyist scores resounding victories on Capital Hill while public office buildings are smoke free. Tobacco industry revenues are added to the GNP while mortality statistics relating to cigarette smoke are computed at the National Institutes of Health.

Instead of efficient and smooth-working government agencies, the bureaucratic form produces agencies that are top-heavy and bottom-lean, where risks are avoided, responsibilities are evaded, people remain up-focused or become in-focused, customers and employees are treated like numbers, procedures become rigid and fixed, and customers do not feel well served. All this in the name of public service?

Guaranteed negative by-products

How can I assert that the negative by-products of bureaucracy stem from using the bureaucratic organizing form?

In 20 years of being invited inside hundreds of public and private sector organizations to help them achieve better customer relations, (I and my associates) have found that the "stuff" we call bureaucracy shows up in every organization that uses the bureaucratic organizing model, and the more stringently the organization applies the organizing principles of bureaucracy—hierarchy, rules, impersonality, organizing into functional units, having an up- or in-focused mission, and employing people based on technical qualifications—the more striking the evidence of bureaucracy.

Top agency officials are the people most eager to find a cure for bureaucracy, because they know that they are wrongly blamed for the bureaucracy. Consider this: If the symptoms of bureaucracies throughout all government agencies are so common and so readily identifiable that we can succinctly list them in this book, then the top officials managers in any given agency *can't have caused them*.

An encouraging word

The heartening news is that when agencies alter their mission, or any of the basic organizing principles of bureaucracy, the negative by-products diminish.

Chapter Four

Fighting symptoms of bureaucracy

Without the awareness that their organizing model is faulty, governmental agencies and businesses have been fighting the *symptoms* of bureaucracy for years.

The immobilizing effects of bureaucracy are clear to those who work in bureaucratic agencies, and to the people the agency serves. Undeniably, every agency has wrestled with one or more of the symptoms of bureaucracy. Many of the solutions being applied are part of new paradigms, such as a customer-focused model, a quality-focused model, or a mission-driven model (see next chapter).

Fighting symptoms provides temporary relief, at best, but does not deal with the "root cause"—the underlying bureaucracy organizing form.

Each of the problems listed below stems from the use of the bureaucratic organizing model; each of the solutions addresses *symptoms* and hence many prove less impactful than if a change were made in the bureaucratic organizing model, or one of its principles.

Red tape

To combat red tape, agencies are trying to:

- re-draft policies, practices, and procedures taking the customer's point of view.

  For example, in Hennepin County, Minnesota, public health inspectors both inspect restaurants and offer owners tips on waste prevention measures. Their advice actually helps the owners maintain or achieve profitable operations while reducing fines and shutdowns.

- empower employees to waive procedural "lapses" when the lapses are not significant.

Inflexibility and unresponsiveness

To combat inflexibility and unresponsiveness, agencies are:

- training and empowering front-line people and managers to be more responsive.

  The Virginia Department of Motor Vehicles, for example, has had greeters in the lobbies of field locations to help make customers feel more at ease when they enter.

- creating cross-functional task teams to put together "fast fixes" to special situations.

  At the U.S. Department of Labor Wage and Hour Division in San Francisco, each of the 140 employees participated in at least two teams in 1990. More than two-thirds of the teams formed were cross-functional joining people in across-job duties, offices, and sub-agencies.

  On the local level, the town government in Rock Hill, South Carolina, created a series of task forces to carry out comprehensive customer service plans.

Not caring about customers

To combat the impression that they don't care about customers, agencies are doing things to indicate that they do care by:

- making policies, practices, and procedures more "customer friendly."

  Supervisors at the Police Department in the city of Hayward, California, tape "words to use" cards next to their phones to remind them of the customer service skills that they've been taught. The Police Department has also returned to the concept of neighborhood beats to enhance services in individual neighborhoods.

- training, coaching, and empowering employees to be conscious of the quality of their outputs and to be flexible and responsive to their internal or external customers.

  At the Washington Area Service Center of the Office of Personnel Management, rework has decreased noticeably. Also requests for reconsideration from job applicants declined in 1989 by more than 75% at OPM—a general indication that applicants were handled correctly throughout the process.

- training, coaching, and empowering employees to be friendly and caring toward their internal and external customers.

  In Oklahoma City, Oklahoma, small easels and mirrors with the popular city slogan, "This City is Me," sit on the desks of employees. The mirrors remind employees to put a smile in their voices when speaking to customers or co-workers.

  The town of Olathe, Kansas, initiated a one-month program to remind employees of the importance of providing fast, effective service and eliminating "bureaucratic runaround." Employees sported buttons that read, "It IS my job." Through departmental meetings they were coached on solving problems themselves when possible, directing inquiries to the right source, and maintaining a good rapport with the public. In addition, each department submitted a list of the 20 questions most commonly asked by customers, to the mayor's office, along with suggested responses. The various lists were approved, printed, and distributed back to the agencies.

- considering the human needs of their customers as well as their administrative needs.

  Following a training program and re-assessment of some policies and procedures, customer representatives at the Georgia Department of Vital Records are responding more rapidly and more accurately to customer requests.

Mistakes

To combat the impression that they are unwilling to admit mistakes, agencies are:

- training employees and managers in the fundamentals of recovery—the art of handling mistakes that their people or the agency makes. Recovery involves accepting responsibility, apologizing, making things right, going at least one extra step, and following up to make certain the customer is satisfied. Recovery helps turn a blunder into a positive memorable customer experience.

  This a now routine at the Virginia Department of Motor Vehicles. In fact, the commissioner's home phone number is listed in the phone book, and in many instances, he handles callers personally.

No innovation

To combat customers' perceptions that their agency is not innovative, or that their products and services are below par, agencies are experimenting with:

- intrapreneurship—an attempt to stimulate entrepreneurial behavior within a heavily bureaucratic agency. Some agencies are seeking entrepreneurial solutions rather than bureaucracy to meet customer needs.

The State of North Carolina funded a housing program run by the Center for Community Self-Help. This $2,000,000 investment resulted in more than $50 million in low-income mortgages by using the marketplace, rather than increasing public spending.

Elsewhere in the state, the city of Winston-Salem created a joint venture with a private-sector firm to build a public parking facility that will not require public funds.

In Georgia, the General Services Administration now sells competitively to both county and city governments and retains its customers by being innovative, easy to work with, and offering competitive prices.

- skunk works—small, usually multi-functional teams, that are formed and challenged to innovate while being free from normal bureaucratic procedures and controls.

In the city of Baltimore, a team within the office of tourism devised an effective program to ensure improved transportation service for customers. Each month a courteous and informed cab driver receives a small cash award from the city. Selected Baltimore cabdrivers and their families were honored with a special day that included breakfast with the mayor, free admission to attractions, sight-seeing, and a dinner. Notice that while the cab drivers in this program are not government employees, their friendliness to customers and visitors created a good impression of the entire city.

- quality programs

The U.S. Internal Revenue Service Center in Ogden, Utah, made marked improvements in processing, reviewing, correcting, and entering tax forms, resulting in more accurate and timely service to taxpayers, and a savings of more than $11 million over a five-year period.

Inaccessibility

To combat customers' observations that agencies are not accessible, some agencies are becoming more accessible by:

- adding "hours open" to their workday.

Traditionally, West Coast residents had to call Washington D.C. agencies before 2:00 PST. Many agencies at all levels of government

have, at the least, installed comprehensive phone systems that direct
callers to the proper office and take after-hours messages with as-
sured call-backs.

- adding 800 numbers to make it easy to reach their agency.

  The Department of Veterans Affairs in Philadelphia recently added
  a nationwide toll-free service for federal government life insurance
  policy holders and their beneficiaries. This service enables customers
  to speak directly to Veterans Affairs employees who are specialists in
  government insurance programs.

- adding to the people who staff their customer contact points,
  so customers do not suffer intolerable waits.

- opening more offices, branches, or other points of contact so
  people can talk face-to-face with human beings if they wish.
  To be more accessible, several state departments of motor
  vehicles have added branches in shopping malls.

  The city of Dallas found that cable TV can be an important tool in
  strengthening communications with customers as well as employees.
  The city developed a video magazine on cable TV. It was hosted by
  the city manager and included question-and-answer sessions, and
  the recognition of outstanding employees.

  Charlotte, South Carolina, has used a regularly scheduled call-in
  show featuring its mayor. Other municipal and county governments
  cities have used cable TV to cover city council meetings and inform
  citizens about issues on the city agendas.

Arrogance and humorless

To combat outsiders' observations that their agency is arrogant and
humorless some agencies are:

- using "straight talk" or humanizing their public communications and, when possible, stopping their senior people from
  being arrogant and humorless.

  The U.S Army and the U.S. Postal Service have had major successes
  in this area. A customer calling to complain to his local post office in
  Chicago was somewhat gratified and totally surprised when he heard
  the respondent say, "Sorry, that's an area we've been botching all
  week. I'll take care of it for you..."

Out of touch with customers

To combat outsiders' observations that they have lost touch with their customers, some agencies will:

- de-centralize and give authority to the managers closest to the customers. As with the other symptom-fighting changes, this change runs in cycles; when faced with "inconsistency" or cost pressures, agencies often find themselves "centralizing" again to restore control.

Fight symptoms internal to the agency

Many bureaucratic agencies are taking the same, one-symptom-at-a-time, approach to reducing the negative effects of bureaucracy on the people in their agencies.

Conflict

To stop departments from being in conflict with one another some agencies are:

- experimenting with "team building" interventions to help their senior people work better together.

  The Department of Defense, particularly the Navy, has made concerted efforts in this area.

  At the state level, Minnesota's efforts to work more effectively in teams has drawn praise and partial funding from several philanthropic organizations.

- requiring that all departments create, and then *nest*, their individual missions within the larger mission. Some are moving away from functional units and reorganizing into multi-disciplinary teams.

- establishing processes to collect feedback for each department from the departments they serve or interact with.

  The Defense Contract Management District Northeast, part of the Defense Logistics Agency, serving 26 field locations in New England and New York state has initiated such procedures.

- linking the departmental manager's performance, and even departmental funding, to the department's success in supporting other departments and helping to remove obstacles rather than being obstacles.

Political in-fighting

To stop political in-fighting some agencies are:

- linking individuals' goals to agency-wide goals ensuring that managers cooperate to achieve their goals.

  At the U.S. Patent and Trademark Office's Public Services and Administration, employees are routinely included in goal setting and monitoring, problem solving and continuous improvement programs.

- collecting peer and subordinate feedback for middle and upper managers.

Turf problems

To minimize turf protection some agencies strive to:

- balance the top-down feedback for manager evaluations with peer-level feedback on issues like collaboration with and support for other departments.

- organize into multi-disciplinary teams focused on customer segments so that the only "turf" is that specific customer segment. The way to protect their turf will be to achieve the mission of satisfying their specific customers.

  The EPA, for example, is moving towards a multi-disciplinary approach to solve environmental problems. In the pulp and paper industry, teams look at clusters of issues and how they can use the statutory requirement of the Clean Air and Clean Water acts to establish new, comprehensive regulations.

Not trusting employees

In bureaucratic agencies with a work environment that traditionally treated employees as though they could not be trusted, did not have good judgment, and would not work hard unless pushed, they are:

- taking steps to change their culture, values, and management style. They realize that nobody has been able to get quality or commitment to customer satisfaction yet from disaffected, underused people who are managed by monitoring, controlling, and disciplining.

The city of Shreveport, Louisiana, started both an employee and a community newsletter. The community newsletter was widely distributed to public locations, such as barber and beauty shops. The employee newsletter helped motivate the employees, and increased communication and the flow of ideas about the city's goals.

Unhealthy stress

Among agencies where the standard work environment includes damaging amounts of unhealthy stress, some agencies are:

- reducing stress through group exercises, soothing music, comfortable lighting, or calming colors.

  The Vital Records Service in Georgia has added hanging plants and artwork on the halls, and replaced cold, metallic chairs with more comfortable cushioned chairs. Employee stress has noticeably decreased, while absenteeism has measurably decreased.

- eliminating subjective, top-down, in-focused, procedurally based personnel assessments and replacing them with objective, mission-related, multi-sourced assessments.

  The U.S. Department of Labor's Wage and Hour Division in the San Francisco Region has had demonstrated success in this area.

- helping their people to remain resilient under high stress by instituting progressive benefit program.

  A variety of agencies on all levels have instituted in-house child care facilities, employee assistance programs to control substance abuse, wellness programs, and smoking cessation courses.

Top heavy

Among agencies where management and staff have grown more and more top-heavy, and the lower ranks tend to be too lean, some agencies are:

- downsizing the middle and upper management ranks.

  This is occurring at the Postal Service and at various branches of the Armed Services.

- re-deploying their people from middle management and staff roles to roles closer to the front line. They have realized that downsizing doesn't do enough to help beef up the lower ranks of the agency, and can result in having too little staff to ensure good customer access, to serve customers well, and/or do a quality job.

Insulated and ill-informed

In bureaucratic agencies that recognize that top managers have become dangerously ill-informed and insulated, they are:

- using employee attitude surveys, customer surveys, "managing by walking around," and employee-focus panels to collect information to inform top mangers.

  In Montgomery County, Ohio, thousands of customers of the Human Services Commission were surveyed to determine the greatest areas of needs. As a result, top officials changed policy. Now, all customers are guaranteed that they will be seen within 15 minutes of their scheduled appointment time, and that Commission employees automatically introduce themselves whether over the phone or in person.

- changing the nature of the decisions that top people make by delegating operating, planning, and even strategic decisions to key people close to the front lines.

- asking senior managers to work the front lines one or two days a month.

  In Rockville, Maryland the County's Executive Officer routinely holds public forums to gauge what the customers see as priorities for the community. Then he meets with the executive council to figure out how to disburse county funds.

- adding new channels of feedback from the front lines.

  Salt Lake City recognized the importance of maintaining the enthusiasm of its employees and the problems inherent in doing so.

  The city initiated training seminars for employees who work with the public and sent memos of recognition from the mayor to city employees at all levels. To maintain the personal touch, the mayor and his chief of staff regularly scheduled brown bag lunches with members of different divisions to discuss department activities.

- putting more emphasis on participative decision making.

  The Patent and Trademark Office's Public Services Administration has achieved immediate positive results with this strategy.

Hoarded information

Among agencies that realize information is hoarded or rationed or used as the basis for power, they are:

- seeking to break up the game by making all non-strategic information widely available.

  The long-standing Freedom of Information Act as well as the ever-increasing distribution of information-generating technology has helped make information in many agencies more accessible. The Department of Agriculture has made a concerted effort in recent years to make information more readily available.

Distorted data

Among agencies recognizing that data has been distorted to prove what is desired, rather than presenting a true picture, some are:

- opening up new channels of information and communication so distortions show up.

Distorted internal communications

In situations where internal communications to employees have become distorted to reflect what the agency would like to be, rather than what it actually is, some agencies are:

- seeking to reverse the process by using "straight talk."

  The Small Business Administration, for example, has been candid about the increasing difficulty and its diminished willingness in defining who should qualify for minority status and thus benefit from the Agency's "8A" program.

Covering up mistakes and failures

When it is clear that mistakes and failures are denied, covered up, or ignored, and responsibility tends to be denied, agencies are:

- working to change their management style from discipline to coaching.

- teaching and promoting "recovery." Others focus on fixing their systems, not their people.

  The Veterans Administration has shown strong initiative in this area.

Diffused decision

When it has become clear that decisions are made by larger and larger groups, making responsibility easily deniable, agencies are:

- introducing the concept of decision sponsors, and tracking decision times.

  This has been initiated at the General Service Administration through their "trail boss" program and implemented throughout federal government procurement activities.

Rigid policies, practices, and procedures

When it has been observed that policies, practices, and procedures are growing more ponderous and more rigid, some agencies are:

- sorting them into red and green rules. "Red" rules are given the weight of law and must be followed. They redefine the "green" rules as guidelines, and empower employees to ignore them when they interfere with mission achievement.

Quantitative over qualitive measurements

The trend in recent years toward less regulation has encouraged many agencies to rely on more informal processes such as guidance toward the accomplishment of goals.

When it becomes clear that quantitative measurements are favored over qualitative measurements causing people to concentrate on quantity rather than quality of output, some agencies are:

- withdrawing the quantitative measurements and replacing them with qualitative measurements.

  Alternatively, some agencies such as the Defense Contract Management District Northeast are using improved statistical methods to continually improve processes, thus ensuring higher quality outputs.

Ignoring human needs

Among agencies where it has become clear that employees and customers feel treated more like numbers than people, and personal issues and human needs are ignored or discounted, they are:

- making special efforts to re-introduce the human component until it balances with the business component.

  The Small Business Administration has announced plans to delegate loan approval to their field offices, which have more first-person contact and understanding of applicants' particular situations. This will represent a shift from the long-standing procedure of head-quarters making all the loan approval decisions based solely on the numbers reflected in the loan packages.

The bureaucratic organizing model is a stable form, and it resists change. The individual steps listed in this chapter are sound interventions and they will work to reduce the negative effects of bureaucracy as well as improve quality, service, and customer and employee satisfaction.

The steps can fail, however, when undertaken individually as attacks on symptoms, because nothing is being done about the root cause... the bureaucratic organizing model. When changes are made one step at a time, the bureaucracy that remains can overwhelm the change, and gradually force it to regress back to "normal." This observation explains why so many changes that have been attempted, based on the best of intentions, have gradually failed.

Interventions are more likely to succeed when they are part of a larger effort designed to replace one or more of the underlying principles of the bureaucratic model. Among the most ambitious of efforts is transformation to the mission-driven form of organizing. Let's turn now to this novel, advanced way for government to serve its customers.

Chapter Five

A new way to organize

There is a better way to organize. If you were creating a new agency, or transforming an existing one, you could organize based on the mission-driven form, instead of the bureaucratic form.

The decline of communism and the end of the Cold War is changing nations and governments at an unprecedented rate. Throughout the world, new governments and agencies are being formed that will be faced with serving their citizens (customers), building the infrastructure, and helping their economies compete in an increasingly global economy.

If those new governments, and their new agencies, adopt the bureaucracy organizing model they may forever trail behind. If, however, the new agencies choose more productive organizing paradigms, they will have the opportunity to bypass the negative by-products of huge bureaucracies.

The mission-driven model is an organizing form that start-ups as well as existing agencies can use. It is *an ambitious organizing form*, however, and represents the furthest possible shift away from the bureaucratic form. The mission-driven form is for agencies seeking to achieve "world class" status. It is not for a typical agency, and I do not recommend that existing agencies convert to such an organizing form. I intentionally offer the following scenario to create a *clear contrast* with the bureaucratic form.

The mission driven model

The mission-driven model combines the process improvement of the total quality management (TQM) model with the customer satisfaction that comes from "customer focused" approaches.

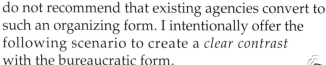

Instead of a formal hierarchy...

The mission-driven model uses a flat organization—seen more frequently, thus far, at the state or local level—in which authority is delegated as near to the front line as possible. Decision authority is granted based on competency, experience, or proven judgement, rather than organizational level.

Remember, the concept of "hierarchy" has some beneficial as well as harmful features. Mission-driven agencies will retain the beneficial features while forsaking the rest. In a nutshell, a mission-driven agency uses hierarchy in a new way:

1. Senior management defines the mission, procures the funding, sets the goals, articulates the vision and strategy, and communicates directly with external agencies.

2. Middle management defines the work teams, allocates resources, removes obstacles, and supports mission achievement.

3. Everyone else organizes into cross-functional teams to achieve the mission.

Management roles change

In bureaucracies, only senior managers need to understand the mission, have a vision, and implement the strategy. This is because senior managers are going to make all of the key decisions and establish the rules under which everyone else will operate.

In mission-driven organizations, on the other hand, the employees closest to the customer will be trained and empowered to make key decisions affecting customer satisfaction. In order for front-line people to make sound decisions, they have to understand and embrace the mission, be clear about the vision, understand the strategy, and be committed to the goals.

Hence, the role of senior management changes. Instead of making all of the key decisions, senior management will set and communicate the mission, strategy, vision, and goals. Its primary role will be to focus and shape the decision-making of people who may be far removed from senior management.

Middle management's job is to establish action teams organized by customer segment or piece of the mission, remove obstacles to the team's success, monitor customer satisfaction, and lead the cheers when the teams make progress toward realizing the vision. Even the middle management level will delegate the key strategic and tactical decisions to the action teams closest to the customers, or those nearest to mission achievement.

The balance of the agency will organize into cross-functional action teams to achieve the mission by defining and then continually improving quality and service. The bulk of the agency will form into teams responsible for serving individual service segments. They will take responsibility for achieving their part of the overall mission by creating extraordinary quality and service.

Continuous improvement

Rather than the bureaucratic strategy of keeping the service constant through rigid application of the idea of "consistency," the action teams will instead strive for "continuous improvement," understanding that they will treat some customers differently to achieve consistently high levels of satisfaction. Continuous improvement is an ongoing process that continuously refines the service to achieve better quality and service.

Customer satisfaction with quality/service is continually monitored to provide feedback to the action teams about customer needs, expectations, and perceptions. The customer feedback is used to encourage change to ensure that the service achieves higher customer satisfaction scores.

In a mission-driven organization—unlike bureaucracy, where the rewards go to the leaders and managers—the rewards go to the individuals or teams that are contributing most to delighting customers or earning public support. Managers will earn recognition for doing their share in establishing optimal missions, strategies, and goals, and for their effectiveness in creating and communicating visions that can be realized by the action teams. The bulk of the rewards and recognition will accrue to the teams who achieve the mission and realize the vision.

Measurement

The *measures* that drive action as well as rewards and recognition will be customer satisfaction measurements (or other mission-related measures derived externally; for example, measures of overall public support).

Mission-driven agencies will drive change and improvement from customer satisfaction measurements. Bureaucratic organizations use internal measures to drive change. These are in-focused measures and are aligned with the in-focused mission.

Mission-driven organizations will also have a different strategy for employee recognition. The mission-driven agency will use internal and external customer satisfaction measurements as the primary determinant of who gets recognized.

Among federal agencies, NASA, the National Science Foundation, and other science-based organizations tend to follow this path.

To recap, hierarchy will be used to establish the mission, and set the initial goals, the strategy, and the original vision. Hierarchy will play a role in monitoring the team results to ensure teams are aligning with the mission, vision, strategy, and goals. As the teams are empowered to achieve the mission, the teams may take on the responsibility of adjusting the strategy, setting their own long-term goals, and refining the vision to better achieve the mission.

When teams are so effective that they can be held totally responsible for their own goals, strategies, and vision, they can be said to be "self directed." Once teams are "self directed," the traditional bureaucratic organizing form's concept of hierarchy will have been totally displaced by the mission-driven concept of empowered teams.

Instead of management by rules...

The mission-driven model uses "empowerment with guidelines." Rules are first divided into "red" rules, which need to be obeyed because they are laws or important ethical or moral issues, and "green" rules, which are within the power of the agency to change, and are converted to "guidelines."

Employees are empowered to make the decisions necessary to improve the quality of their output, or to do what it takes to satisfy the customer. They have guidelines to use, but competent employees are empowered to abandon the guidelines if it does not result in improving quality or satisfying the customer. This makes it possible to give priority to achieving the mission when it makes sense to do so, rather than "going by the book."

Guidelines and other levels of empowerment will largely replace rules.

In bureaucracies, people are empowered to make decisions based on their level within the agency's hierarchy. In mission-driven agencies, people are empowered to make decisions based on their experience, skill, training, or capability, rather than their level. This means that an individual in an entry-level position can gradually become more and more empowered to make decisions without being forced to rise in organizational level.

Kaset International's training program, "Managing Extraordinary Service" and "Managing Moments of Truth," identifies five levels of empowerment.

Person/Team	Not Serious	Fairly Serious	Very Serious
High	**Level 1** Totally Empowered	**Level 2** Post-Action	**Level 3** Guidelines
Medium	**Level 2** Post-Action	**Level 3** Guidelines	**Level 4** Pre-Action
Low	**Level 3** Guidelines	**Level 4** Pre-Action	**Level 5** Not Empowered

Seriousness of Consequence

Level 5: Not empowered

In situations where the potential
negative outcome of a poor decision
is of great consequence to the agency;
or in situations in which the individual lacks the experience, skill, training, or capability to make good decisions.
At this level of empowerment, the individual either gets management to decide
or follows specific rules, thus eliminating
individual decision-making. This is the
normal level at which people operate in
bureaucratic agencies.

Level 4: Pre-action empower-
ment

In situations where the individual is
learning, practicing, or proving his/
her ability to make good mission-driven
decisions, or where the consequences of a mistake
are more than the agency is willing to risk. In these situations, the
individual comes to an "empowerer" with his/her own decision
before actually implementing the decision. This allows opportunity
for confirmation or corrective coaching.

Level 3: Empowerment with guidelines

In situations where the individual is entrusted to make
mission-achieving decisions within guidelines. As long at the individual stays within the guidelines, the individual is empowered to
make decisions that, in other agencies, might be reserved for supervisors or managers. This level of empowerment makes it possible for front-line people to make mission-achieving decisions,
thereby satisfying customers, without having to chase up the line to
get managerial approval.

Level 2: Post-action empowerment

In situations where the individual has the experience, skill, or
training to make good decisions, or for situations where a poor decision (relative to the mission) is not of the most serious consequence. At this level, the individual proceeds to make decisions, but

periodically goes over them (after they are made) with an empowerer, as an opportunity for coaching and further development.

Level 1: Total empowerment

For individuals who are experienced, skilled, trained, or have proven capable of making sound mission-achieving decisions. At this level of empowerment, individuals are empowered to make decisions that go outside of guidelines without further approval or post-action review. Notice also that empowerment is granted by situation or type of decision, i.e. no one individual is fully empowered on all situations.

In summarizing the principle of empowerment, notice that the mission-driven agency deals with levels of empowerment, rather than levels of management.

In flat organizations, where authority levels are limited or non-existent, individuals still learn and achieve personal growth through empowerment. Individual accomplishment and experience contribute to growth in empowerment, related to the mission.

This contrasts sharply with the bureaucratic form, which often links growth (in levels within the agency) to support of internal objectives.

In the bureaucratic form, achieving higher levels generally takes people farther and farther away from the customer (the trenches). The mission-driven model gives individuals the ability to grow, learn, achieve more responsibility, earn higher income, and stay close to the customer—where the action is.

Instead of an up-focused or in-focused mission...

The mission-driven model has a *customer-focused mission*, either through extraordinary service, accomplishing its charter, or innovation. The agency trusts that if it achieves its mission, it will earn public support and thus satisfy those who chartered it.

What's the difference between an in-focused mission and a customer-focused mission? A customer-focused mission has the power to energize, motivate, and guide ALL employees in the agency, whereas only a few people in an agency would jump out of bed each morning eager to get to work to prolong the life of the agency or assure that the hierarchy be maintained.

In-focused missions create agencies with two missions, where top management is interested in achieving the internal mission (increased funding, added staffing, additional turf), and the mission of the rest of the agency is to perform the "public" mission and satisfy the public enough so that the internal mission can be realized.

A customer-focused mission will be expressed in terms of the customer, and will be measured in terms of direct or indirect feedback from customers. An in-focused mission does not address the customer.

Customer-focused missions

Here are some examples of customer-focused missions:

Kaset International's mission is: *"To help organizations achieve extraordinary customer relations."*

In the private sector, a customer-focused mission for a bank might be: *"To create and maintain customer banking relationships that our customers feel are personally and financially rewarding."*

If this bank achieves its mission, then growth is assured, and because loyal customers are less rate-sensitive, the probability of good profits is high. It is important to notice that profits and growth are by-products, and the mission is customer satisfaction.

An example of a customer-focused mission for a government agency might be: *"To help each eligible citizen acquire and maintain safe and responsible driving privileges."* Notice that this mission statement puts the agency in a supportive and collaborative relationship with the citizen. It aligns with what the citizens want. It moves away from the old bureaucratic paradigm where it seems to some customers that the licensing agency is looking for ways to avoid licensing drivers.

Customer-focused missions have the power to guide, energize, and motivate employees at all levels of the agency. Having a customer-focused mission makes it possible to have an agency that is totally aligned with the mission, avoiding the bureaucratic result of having split missions, or worse yet, apathetic alignment on an up-focused mission.

Sometimes, officials from bureaucratic agencies think they already have customer-focused missions. They point to the agency charter, which says something like, "We serve the public who come first with us," and they proclaim, "We're dedicated to public service."

The distinction between an in-focused mission and a customer-focused mission shows up best in the trenches. When you truly have a customer-focused mission, then employees will "strongly agree" with the statement, "The number one priority with both employees and management is satisfying the customer."

If you have an in-focused mission masquerading as a customer-focused mission, then employees will be ambivalent, or they will agree with a statement like: "While we talk a lot about customer satisfaction, the most important thing to management is perpetuation" (or garnering favorable press, collecting kudos from Congress, or avoiding complaints).

The primary measures that define agency success will be based on customer satisfaction, rather than in-focused measures that will benefit the agency itself, such as justifying its existence, attempting to build a constituency, holding internal inquiries, and always spending all of its budget.

If your mission is timely delivery of service, then you will measure customers' perceptions of your service delivery and judge your agencies performance on the results. If your mission is customer satisfaction, then you will measure customer satisfaction and judge your agency's performance on those scores. You will prove the truth of the cliché, "What you measure is what you get."

If top management's mission is up-focused or in-focused, then eventually the entire agency will adopt the up-focused or in-focused mission. The only way to achieve a customer-focused, or quality-focused mission is for top officials to adopt and live out the customer-focused or quality-focused mission.

Instead of organizing employees by the type of work they do...

The mission-driven model leads to organizing by multi-disciplinary, or cross-functional teams to serve specific objectives or customer segments, and not by bunching up employees by what they do, such as procurement, field representation, auditing, or computer programming.

Multi-functional teams will replace specialization by job function. The mission-driven agency will seek to eliminate functional "walls" or "boundaries" that need to be crossed to achieve the mission. The goal is to be sure that every resource or skill that the team will need to continually improve service, quality, or both, is available on the team—without having to cross any agency boundary.

This principle may appear to produce internal inefficiencies, but it does not. Cross-functional teams do not need the layers of managers and administrative staff that make bureaucracies top-heavy. Because the teams are committed to missions that are customer focused, they aim to optimize mission achievement rather than the in-focused goal of minimizing front-line staff.

Cross-functional teaming is in stark contrast to the bureaucratic form, which groups people by the work they do or the training they've had, with the goal of creating efficiencies that benefit the agency. This is another example of the difference between what is optimized in an in-focused mission and what is optimized in a customer-focused mission-driven agency.

Instead of being purposely impersonal...

The mission-driven model balances both human and mission concerns. The mission-driven agency manifests caring and concern for employees and for customers, in balance with concern for quality in the operational aspects. Agencies whose missions are to achieve extraordinary customer service are learning that customer satisfaction is strongly influenced by human issues such as how much the agency seems to "care" about its customers.

> In Bryan, Texas, city officials devised a plan to both revitalize customer confidence in local government and ensure that the government would seem more personal to its customers. The town used city employees in the development of public communication tools. Advertisements and press releases highlighted city employees in features covering their responsibilities. The city also increased the frequency of community service and special events, and increased recognition of accomplishments by city employees. In the words of one official, "These strategies helped Bryan residents recognize that growth and change are not to be feared and that stagnation is the town's real enemy."

Achieving extraordinary customer service requires treating each customer in the way that the customer wants and needs to be treated. The extraordinary flexibility and fluidity required of the mission-driven agency are implemented by empowered people and flexible policies, practices, and procedures.

The mission-driven agency depends on its *employees* for the achievement of its mission. Again, this contrasts with the bureaucratic form, which depends primarily on *management* for the achievement of its in-focused mission. In a mission-driven agency, employees need to be committed to the mission and loyal to the agency, for the agency to achieve its mission.

Employee loyalty, like customer loyalty, depends on the agency attending to the human needs of the individual. This reality can be stated both positively and negatively. If the agency doesn't "care" about its employees, it will be difficult to get the employees to "care" about its mission or its customers. Conversely, an agency that "cares" about its employees will have employees who are more likely to "care" about its mission and customers.

Instead of hiring based solely on specific skills or prior training...

The mission-driven model suggests hiring for both professional skills *and* the desired human attributes. Mission-driven agencies will seek to hire for such human attributes as "attitude," "desire," "commitment," and "caring," as well as the necessary functional skills. The agency is concerned with the human needs of both its customers and its employees.

Both customers and employees will be affected by the human facets of new employees joining the agency. Mission-driven agencies cannot allow their mission to be sabotaged by employees who think that government or the world "owes" them a living, or whose interpersonal skills make it intolerable to work around them. This is not to say that mission-driven agencies will be arbitrary or discriminatory in their hiring. It is clearly possible to be non-discriminatory in hiring, and still give strong consideration to human factors that support achieving the mission.

The bureaucratic model may succeed in reducing discrimination by rigidly testing only functional attributes. The impact of employees with terrible work attitudes and abominable interpersonal skills, however, is damaging to both fellow employees and customers.

The bureaucratic form also allows for virtually total job security in some cases (i.e., tenure) and in other cases offers substantial protection against arbitrary dismissal (e.g., civil service). It has never been shown that providing job security produces better public service from government workers.

The mission-driven agency will provide job security linked to the individual's contribution to mission achievement. Individuals who contribute to mission achievement will be highly valued and will earn job security as a by-product. Security comes with achieving the mission—achieving quality output or delighting customers. Employees are protected from arbitrary termination, and termination is largely reserved for those unable or unwilling to satisfy customers or produce quality output.

Individuals who act directly or indirectly as barriers to mission achievement will have little job security. The mission-driven agency will base performance assessments on a range of input, from teammates, teamleaders, and where possible, from direct or indirect customer feedback.

Instead of a predisposition to grow top-heavy and bottom-lean...

The mission-driven model aims to create one unified team—perhaps made up of many smaller teams—with everyone focused on the same mission. There are none of the bureaucratic payoffs for high-level bloat, and lots of incentives to stay lean and focused on the mission.

There is a "line" in agencies that divides management and staff positions from lower ranking positions. I've noticed that the people "above the line" in agencies tend to think that good management involves keeping the staff "below the line" as small as possible.

In the evolving bureaucratic agency, two simultaneous forces are at work. One is the tendency for the number of people "above the line" to grow. The other is the tendency of top management to re-duce staff "below the line." In the fully mature bureaucracy, this results in the outcome I describe as top-heavy, bottom-lean.

The number of people below the line may not actually shrink, but it is considered good "productivity" if the staff below the line grows more slowly than does agency funding. The effect of the top-heavy bottom-lean phenomenon is to cause service to gradually deterio-rate until the agency performs poorly in terms of customer satis-faction or mission achievement.

Because hierarchy in the mission-driven model is flattened and all employees have the same mission-driven focus, the predisposi-tion to grow top-heavy and bottom-lean is all but eliminated.

Some cite the Tennessee Valley Authority as having made progress in this area.

Contrasting models

The ideal form of the mission-driven agency is almost directly an-tithetical to the bureaucracy organizing form, and each of their or-ganizing principles seems to be almost the opposite of the other form. All of the principles of the mission-driven form are aligned and interconnected, just as are all of the components of the bu-reaucratic form. Organizations that have attempted to change have observed that it is not necessary to adopt every element of the mission-driven form to experience a huge relief from bureaucracy.

When you change only one of the components of the bureau-cratic form, however, you create tension and misalignment. Gradually, each of the other organizing principles has to adjust to become aligned with the piece you have changed, or else the com-ponent will return to its original state to resolve the tension.

The agency will feel most secure and unconflicted when all of the principles of the bureaucratic form or the mission-driven form are adopted. When you adopt only some of the principles, you can ex-pect that some tension will arise.

The mission-driven form of organization adopts an externally-focused mission, creates a very flat organization, uses a modified concept of hierarchy, uses guidelines and other levels of empower-ment to largely replace rules, balances business needs with human needs for customers and employees, and uses cross-functional teams to replace work units organized by function. It also hires employees based on human skills as well as professional skills, and bases job security on success in mission achievement.

Chapter Six

Modifying the basic components of bureaucracy

A more powerful way to reduce bureaucracy than fighting symptoms one at a time—but a far less rigorous approach than full application of the mission-driven form—is to modify one or more of the basic principles of the bureaucratic form. This does not require the adoption of a new organizing model, but it can bring more relief than fighting bureaucratic symptoms one at a time.

Modifying one or more basic principles of the bureaucratic form can significantly reduce bureaucracy. There are many places to start.

An agency could choose to change its mission

Changing from an in-focused, or up-focused mission to a mission focused on service quality might require legislation to modify the relationship between the agency and the legislators that charter, sponsor, and fund it. Any agency (whether at the federal, state or local level) that is subject to continual oversight (meddling—by multiple bosses, with different, and often conflicting agendas) cannot help but become "up-focused," immobilized, and ineffectual.

*The Environmental Protection Agency, for example, receives oversight and budgetary appropriations **from 18 different congressional committees.***

Having a service quality mission requires measurements based on customer feedback. The sponsors of the agency would have to allow the new measurements to take priority over current measurements which gauge in-focused goals. Once employees at all levels understand that the agency *does* have a new number-one priority, the agency has the opportunity to align the entire agency around the new mission.

Let the magic begin

When the people in an agency become aligned around a customer-focused mission, magic seems to happen. Not only do the bureaucratic symptoms fade away, but the employees, the customers they serve, and the public at large reach new levels of satisfaction.

The mission is the single most important principle of the organizing model. If the mission becomes truly customer focused, it will be difficult for any of the remaining bureaucratic principles to work against the achievement of the mission.

Conversely, if the mission were to remain "up-focused" (e.g., satisfy the legislature, Congress, or the city council), then it will be difficult to genuinely change any of the other organizing principles of the bureaucratic model. Admittedly, it is a special challenge for federal agencies, where top leaders change so frequently, to avoid reverting to an "up-focused" mission with every leadership change.

An agency could convert to a flat structure

An agency can convert from a hierarchical structure to a flat agency structure by reorganizing to reduce layers, and redeploying people to focus on delighting customers, achieving higher quality, or both.

Customer feedback will make continuous improvement possible, but success depends on employees who are committed to service quality improvement, trained to work in teams, and trained to apply problem-solving skills to those customer situations that are most important to your customers.

In bureaucratic agencies, the amount of training and development an employee gets usually is based on their level. Managers make the key decisions and "get things done," so managers get the training. When you are seeking to debureaucratize and empower lower-level employees to solve service and quality problems, you'll need to give those employees far more training than bureaucracies are accustomed to giving to lower-level people.

One of the barriers to agency change efforts is this traditional allocation of training by level. Senior managers can find themselves stuck in the old bureaucratic way of thinking. They may resist investing in the growth and development of what they think of as lower-level people. Problem solving is a process that almost anyone can learn, yet few know how to do it well unless they've been trained. Teamwork improves incredibly once people have been trained in the processes that make teams work effectively together. *An agency could further reduce hierarchy* by doing more participative management, and moving toward consensus decision making.

An agency could convert from managing by "rules" to empowering with guidelines

An agency that relies on "mandates," or "edicts," or "rules" is behaving in a manner that adds to the bureaucracy. Rules preclude the use of individual judgment and strict adherence to the rules may unintentionally result in compromising the mission.

It is debureaucratizing to participatively arrive at permissions, protections, and guidelines that people can use to govern their own actions. Managers then can replace control with observing and coaching, and they can evaluate team or individual performance based on mission achievement rather than rule conformance.

When non-managers get to play a role in shaping the guidelines that will be used and are empowered to put aside the guidelines when the mission is endangered, they are likely to "buy in" to the

guidelines and use them when they work to achieve the mission. Individuals can be held responsible for "pre-action" approval before abandoning guidelines in critical decision areas. For less critical decisions, "post-action review" can be authorized to allow for coaching and management guidance.

Pre-action approvals are useful when a decision is too critical to delegate. Sometimes the person isn't yet prepared by experience or training to make the decision. In these cases, requiring a pre-action approval can provide a good opportunity for developmental coaching.

An agency could reorganize away from specialized functional departments...

...and toward multi-disciplinary teams organized by customer segment, service type, or product segment. Front-line people, for example, could be organized as natural work units, cross-functional teams, or multi-disciplinary teams, and be responsible for creating the desired product quality or dazzling customer service that is their mission.

In customer-driven agencies, front-line people won't be standing around waiting for instructions from above. They will know what's needed, and they'll be "empowered" to do it. Such teams are motivated by the job itself, now that they understand how their work supports the mission. They are motivated by the "growth" that they've attained as they've learned the skills needed to do their job at the highest level of skill and the additional developmental skills attendant with self-management.

Team members are also motivated by the "responsibility" that has become theirs as the multi-disciplinary team rather than management becomes responsible for the mission. They are motivated by the "recognition" that comes from being from being part of a winning team. Multi-disciplinary teams tend to have more fun on the job and don't experience the damaging stress that comes from being alienated from management, fearful of being disciplined, and dehumanized by being treated like a unit of production.

An agency could decide not to be purposely "impersonal"

An agency could decide to increase the emphasis on the "human" component in employee relations and customer relations. It could add choices for employees and for customers to avoid treating everyone equally, and strive instead for equal satisfaction.

The agency could still maintain the requisite variety of responses to ensure that both employees and customers are treated as individuals, with unique needs and circumstances.

This does not suggest that polices, practices, and procedures will be implemented capriciously. It does mean that the agency will offer enough choices and alternatives to its customers and employees so that each person can choose the particular solution he or she needs.

I understand the personal, legal, procedural, legislative, and historical barriers to making changes of the magnitude described above. I have no illusions that the barriers would be easy to overcome. I suggest that the alternative—continuing on with an increasingly ineffectual form of government, which fails to satisfy an increasingly restless populace—is far worse than facing up to the challenge.

The Japanese bureaucracy

As a side note, some Japanese business organizations in the private sector have inadvertently moderated several principles of bureaucracy, and demonstrated how effectively organizations with a modified bureaucratic form can compete with organizations based on the traditional bureaucratic model. While they do not seem to have taken purposeful aim at replacing the bureaucratic organizing form, nevertheless, the most successful Japanese organizations have:

- replaced up-focused missions with missions focusing on quality or customer satisfaction that serve to align managers and employees.
- moderated the worst effects of hierarchy by their cultural inclination toward consensus seeking.
- moderated the bureaucratic effects of "specialization" by bringing different specialties together in project teams, and inducing technical specialists to subordinate their craft to the larger mission.

Because of the clear and aligning mission, departments are more likely to work harmoniously with other departments toward the larger mission, whether or not cross-functional teams are used.

The most successful Japanese companies are dominating the global marketplace by having modified the bureaucratic organizing model. I predict that successful businesses of the future will be those that substantially or totally eliminate bureaucracy and replace it with a different organizing model.

Canadian government

In government, modifying the bureaucratic form has also proven successful. In Canada, for example, Otto Brodtrick made a study of the best performing Canadian governmental agencies. Within each of the eight best performing agencies named, one can find evidence of one or more departures from the traditional bureaucratic model, moving, at least slightly, toward the mission-driven model. Some agencies took pains to be less hierarchical. Some empowered their front-line people. Some intentionally added some "human" to their transactions. Each of the best-performing agencies changed the focus of their mission from being in-focused or up-focused, to being citizen-focused or quality-focused.

The study, titled *Attributes of Well-Performing Organizations*, was originally extracted from the report of the Auditor General of Canada to the House of Commons. Reading the report, one observes that each agency had fewer of the negative effects of bureaucracy. It was also clear that the bureaucracy was reduced as a by-product of some other effort or change, rather than being itself the target of the change. The well-performing agencies *had found ways to reduce bureaucracy without taking serious aim at the bureaucratic organizing model*. Imagine how extraordinary the performance of a governmental agency could be when it sets out to change one or more of its organizing principles!

Thus far, we have talked about debureaucratizing by:

- fighting the symptoms,
- starting up a new agency using the ambitious mission-driven form, and
- changing an existing agency by changing one or more of the basic principles of the bureaucratic organizing model.

In the next chapter we will examine what could happen if an *existing* agency adopted a new organizing model to replace the bureaucratic organizing model.

Chapter Seven

Adopting a new organizing form

The most powerful way to reduce or eliminate the effects of bureaucracy is to adopt a new organizing form.

If the agency has an important customer-service component in its mission, it could choose a *customer-focused* mission, and then make the agency mission driven. If the agency's public support or citizen satisfaction depends solely on the quality of their services or processes—and customer satisfaction is a natural and predictable by-product of high quality service or processes—then it could choose a *quality-focused* mission, and proceed to make the agency mission driven.

In either case—customer-focused or quality-focused—employing the mission-driven model necessitates changing *each* of the organizing principles of the bureaucratic organizing form.

Getting started

Suppose you agree that adopting the mission-driven organizing form would "supercharge" your agency. Perhaps you do not have all the resources necessary for the task, or are not in the right position to make these changes. Nevertheless, you would like to begin thinking along the lines of the mission-driven model, and get others to do so as well. This chapter offers a road map, including desirable outcomes and steps during transition.

The outcomes are straightforward

The types of outcomes you would seek to achieve are straightforward, and represent a reversal of the six components of bureaucracy as discussed in Chapter Three.

1. to replace the in-focused mission with a quality or customer-focused mission that everyone in the agency will support. A customer-focused mission makes possible the evolution of a single, unified, and harmonious team, with everyone committed to the same outcome.

You fool yourself if you think you can reduce bureaucracy by substituting one in-focused set of goals for another in-focused set of goals. In other words, you don't debureaucratize by mounting a campaign for less staff, or higher visibility, or getting increased funding. These are examples of the kinds of goals that led your agency to bureaucracy in the first place.

2. to end up with a flat agency structure, with people at the front lines committed to their role in mission achievement. Those who work on internal processes will be employing quality tools to continually improve the quality of their output. Those who handle customers will be working to continually improve customer satisfaction with customer service.

The shift away from a many-leveled hierarchy to a flat agency with the fewest practical levels moves toward decision authority based on experience, training, skill, and closeness to the customer.

3. front-line people organized into multi-disciplinary teams, where everyone on the team is aligned with the quality or customer-focused mission. This ensures that people have to cross the fewest possible departmental boundaries to achieve their quality or service mission.

Motivation results from employees' participation as team members. The teams are responsible for creating the desired level of quality or customer service.

4. a balance of concern for the business and the human components of customer transactions. This assures that the human needs of the customer, as well as the administrative needs, are met. It creates loyal and motivated employees who are more likely to be committed to their work and the agency's mission. No longer feeling like numbers, both customers and employees have a renewed faith in the agency.

5. to select your employees for their interpersonal skills as well as their business skills, so you will have people who value satisfying internal and external customers, and will demonstrate good teamwork.

6. to make mission achievement matter to your front-line people, their supervisors, and managers, and to make quality or customer service a condition of continued employment.

Step by step

The steps you take during the transition to the mission-driven model are each, by themselves, not too difficult. The extent of the transformation, however, makes it challenging, and requires extreme patience. The following is a condensed overview of the steps an agency would take to make the conversion from bureaucracy to *any* different organizing form, which includes the mission-driven form.

Create and articulate frequently a new customer-focused mission

Your goal for a mission statement is something so simple, direct, and compelling that you can describe it in one or two sentences. When you get it right, everyone in the agency can quote it, align with it, and use it to test their individual initiatives and decisions.

Even without being able to meet the above tests for the optimal mission statement, the city of Cleveland, was able to reverse a long-standing negative image. The "New Cleveland" campaign had three basic objectives:

- *to identify and document Cleveland's strengths and continuing development,*
- *to communicate these matters in a credible, creative, and effective manner commensurate with the quality of the city itself,*
- *to restore and enhance local, regional, national, and international confidence in Cleveland.*

Teach everyone their new roles

Enlist everyone in the fight against the negative attributes of the bureaucratic model that have crept into the culture. Teach everyone in the agency to recognize bureaucratic behaviors so they can stop using them, and help others to stop using them as well.

The purpose of this step is to help your people resist backsliding from, say, the new and unfamiliar customer-focused model to the more familiar bureaucratic model.

Teach customer-contact employees

The employees require skills to make customers satisfied, happy, delighted, or even dazzled.

Dazzling customers isn't hard, but it requires some special skills. Teach internal support people that everyone has a customer, and that internal customer satisfaction is essential before you can expect the agency to fully satisfy external customers.

Teach the employees who are responsible for the quality of your internal processes

These employees need skills to produce output that satisfies their customers. Quality tools have been successfully taught to employee groups throughout the world. Front-line people, working in teams, supported by a "total quality management" environment, can continually improve the quality of their output.

Ford Motor Company made quality "Job Number One" and was able to transform itself in less than five years.

In the public sector, the Virginia Department of Motor Vehicles has, in part, transformed itself by focusing on the needs of its customers and adapting itself accordingly.

Change the way managers deal with the front line

Use training and coaching to convert managers from using a disciplinary strategy to a coaching strategy. Customer-satisfying quality or service requires the kind of front-line commitment that is not produced by control and discipline.

Senior management will still be important in terms of defining the mission, choosing the strategy, marshalling the necessary resources, and communicating the vision. Their overall responsibility and their role change relatively little, except in terms of making "rules" or constraining operational decisions. To achieve extraordinary quality or service for your customers, senior and middle management need to change the way they view "the employees." Senior managers also need to stop believing that they can "control" the execution of the mission at or near the front lines. They will need to substitute empowerment—giving permission, protection, and coaching—for control.

> *Years back, as the ill-fated Penn Central Railroad offered sharply declining service, late trains, dirty cars, and inadequate air conditioning. Once-friendly conductors became noticeably rude and disinterested to passengers. They became that way, in part, because they were on the front line and were the only Penn Central employees that passengers encountered. In short, they got all the abuse.*

In both the public and private, front-line employees often take the blame for a poor organization. (Rudeness and poor morale is seldom an employee problem.)

In the hotel industry, as another example, front desk personnel are generally paid less than back office personnel but are more responsible for the perception of service. They set the image and the mood. The finest room and most delectable food won't bring customers back if they have been treated rudely or think they didn't get proper service.

Change the way middle managers manage their segments of the agency

Middle managers need to evolve strategies for managing internal and external customer service. To evolve a strategy requires creating, communicating, and implementing the strategy. To carry out this process requires innovation and initiatives that have not been highly valued within the bureaucratic form, but which are vital in making the agency flexible and responsive to customers.

Middle managers will play a vital role by organizing, communicating the strategy, allocating resources wisely, and doing their part to bring the vision to life. Their role also changes from being "controlling" managers to becoming "coaches" and obstacle removers.

Get senior management committed to being mission driven

When senior managers have the opportunity to get out from under the bureaucratic rat race, and become skilled in "management by walking around," they invariably become imbued with a new or renewed sense of mission.

This step requires that the governmental entity responsible for the agency empower the agency to depart from the bureaucratic organizing form and to adopt a mission-driven form. This step also suggests that the empowering entity hold the subordinate agency heads responsible for meeting mission-driven goals and measurements, such as quality, customer satisfaction, or public support, rather than traditional bureaucratic measurements.

Monitor your progress internally

Employee perception and attitude surveys, added to employee-focus panels, can give feedback to those responsible for managing the transition. Use the initial employee measurements as a benchmark, and measure periodically throughout the transition as a progress check.

Reorganize the front-line people

Your front-line people need to be part of multi-disciplinary teams focused on projects, products, outcomes, or customer segments. Do your best to have all of the various skills or disciplines necessary on each team to satisfy virtually every need for service, quality, or outcome, without having to cross departmental boundaries.

The people at this level will organize into teams and change from being supervisor driven to being mission driven. By virtue of experience, capability, and training, they will earn responsibilities and authority barely dreamt of in the traditional bureaucracy.

The teams will be responsible for some segment of customers, or some service, and will have the responsibility and authority to improve quality and service with the goal of maximizing customer satisfaction or outcome quality. If the nature of your agency dictates that you focus on quality improvement, the training to accomplish this is readily available from a variety of suppliers. Training is one of the easiest parts of the change effort because front-line people have a lot to gain. Their work life becomes much more interesting, varied, and challenging as they are allowed to use the full range of talents that they bring to work.

Yet, sometimes it is difficult to "enroll" the front-line people in the effort. You may be starting with an alienated work force, but they *can be* won over.

Re-deploy old mission supporters

The people supporting an up-focused or in-focused mission need to be re-deployed as soon as possible. You risk pulling the agency in opposite directions if you don't dismantle much of the apparatus supporting up-focused, or in-focused goals.

Also, the old bureaucratic form may have left you top-heavy and bottom-lean. Downsizing only deals with the top-heavy problem. Re-deploying the people whose positions would otherwise be out of place or unnecessary will allow you to avoid being bottom-lean. You also need to get senior managers out of the bureaucratic mire. Dissolving the in- and up-focused sub-units will free people from the memo-and-meeting rat race so they can actually confront the issues or meet the people the agency was created to serve.

Make supporting the mission matter

Make it matter that front-line people, supervisors, middle managers, and senior managers support the quality or customer-focused mission. Three subtasks will help here:

- Use the customer satisfaction measurements that you install. They are valuable in evaluating customer-contact people and teams responsible for producing quality outputs.

- Create consequences by changing the reinforcers. Promotions, raises, rewards, and recognitions can all be realigned to reinforce the desired customer-satisfaction behavior.

- Install new peer ratings and upward assessments so that managers get feedback from above, below, and from their peers. Use the same tools for people working in teams. This will ensure that team members and managers stop focusing just on satisfying the boss, as in a hierarchy, and focus more on supporting their peers, removing obstacles, and supporting those who report to them.

Make policies, practices, and procedures customer friendly

Open up new lines of communication to get input from customers, suppliers, and employees on their satisfaction with policies, practices, and procedures.

In-focused agencies generally create policies, practices, and procedures designed to meet internal goals. To support a mission-focused agency, the policies, practices, and procedures need to be rewritten until they are the way that customers would ask you to write them "customer friendly."

The New York Department of Labor took a long, hard look at how they could deliver their services the way customers wanted. As a result, the agency reorganized so that a variety of services, combining federal, state, local and volunteer programs, were all offered under one roof at four different locations.

Enlist the support of internal consultants and change agents

It is bureaucratic to become dependent on external consultants. It is mission-driven to bring the knowledge and skills needed inside the agency and become self-sufficient and autonomous.

Insist that any consultants who guide you are willing and able to transfer their knowledge to your people so the change processes can be undertaken internally. I have witnessed change efforts that failed because the agency did not have the expertise to plan and manage the effort on their own, and they did not seek professional guidance. I've also seen change efforts fail because the outside consultants were generalists and didn't have experience with planning and guiding organizational change efforts.

Agencies seeking to transform themselves are best served by a single supplier that can supply the entire system of support: consulting to define the plan, training to support the plan, and customer feedback to track progress.

As you seek help, check with the existing customers of any consulting organization you are considering. Ask the references how successful the change effort is, and whether the result lives up to what the consultant led them to expect. Also, look for proof that the external consultants have created independence in the referenced agency. Seek multiple references. Ask the consultants for their entire customer list, and then you choose which clients to call.

The most successful change efforts I have seen are those where the outside consultants transferred their knowledge and expertise to inside consultants who became responsible for implementation. By having outside consultants plan and guide the effort, you avoid getting caught up in the internal power politics that occur when internal consultants are used to plan the change effort.

By having inside consultants implement the change effort, the agency is taking responsibility for its own fate and takes ownership of the transformation.

Chapter Eight

Getting feedback from where it counts

Check your progress in building public support or in satisfying customers by collecting feedback from the agencies' customers.

In years of working with both public- and private-sector organizations, I have yet to find one agency that is collecting the kind of customer information useful to increase customer satisfaction. From what I know of the successful Japanese private-sector organizations, I have yet to discover one that *isn't* gathering the customer feedback they need to satisfy customers.

Japanese organizations, both public and private, routinely collect substantial feedback from their customers and use that information to improve services, products, and their delivery. For some reason, North American as well as European organizations don't tend to collect such information, or if they do, they rarely give it the weight it deserves.

Collecting feedback

If your mission is to serve and satisfy the public, how can you tell how you are doing without collecting feedback from the public?

You may be getting little or no regular customer feedback. Most agencies that I have worked with personally have had no regular system of collecting feedback from customers. A few occasionally use some type of field survey, which offers some indication of how satisfied the customers are, but often the information is global and directed at senior management.

In a global survey, only a few questions are typically devoted to issues of customer satisfaction, and those are generally somewhat cursory. A report written for senior management seldom contains the level of detail that would be useful in identifying specific customer dissatisfaction issues, and would not be helpful to teams focused on improving specific elements of quality, or customer service.

Some organizations find negative customer feedback so discomforting that they react to it by "shooting the messenger." In one case, which I will disguise somewhat to protect the embarrassed, I was shown three surveys, done over eight years, by three different research firms. The earliest report contained good questions, a high-quality rating scale, and poor customer satisfaction ratings. They fired the firm and buried the report. Senior management said that the report conflicted with constant feedback from the front lines that customers were satisfied.

The second report contained good questions, a slightly less discriminating rating scale, but even more rigorous and professional survey protocol. The results were slightly higher, but still extremely low. The scores, however, were interwoven with narrative that made the low scores sound almost terrific. In this instance, the research was sound, but the interpretation was clearly designed to present bad news in the most favorable possible light. The second research firm wasn't told that it was fired, but it wasn't used again.

The third report contained leading questions and a primitive rating scale that invites distortion of the results—a three-point scale, with the customer able to choose between very satisfied, somewhat satisfied, and terribly dissatisfied. The customer only had three choices, and the top two were combined to give a score that showed that 82 percent of the customers were somewhat or very satisfied. Another way to view the same information (which was not written in the report), was that 65 percent of all customers were less than satisfied, and 18 percent of them were "terribly" dissatisfied.

The report was glowing about the improvement in customer satisfaction that had been achieved since the prior reports, with no mention of the distortion caused by the questions or the rating scale. Not surprisingly, the third report was well received by senior management, and was the first of the three reports that was circulated. As I understood it, the third market research firm was well thought of and would do any future research the organization required.

If you shoot the messengers who bring bad news, you ensure that you'll only get good news, and a steady diet of only "good news" can cause executives to become insulated. The mission-driven agency can't afford to disguise the truth, whereas the bureaucratic agency tends to use whatever data will support the supposition that it's doing a good job.

You'll also need to change the way that negative customer feedback is dealt with inside the agency. Start viewing customer dissatisfaction as something "valuable," because it drives improvement. Begin to view customer feedback in general as "diagnostic," rather than as a performance measure. If you keep shooting the messenger, pretty quickly you'll only get good news, and improvement becomes impossible.

What kind of data are you getting?

The information you get currently is almost certainly quantitative. Quantitative studies are used when a lot of data is being collected. By making the survey quantitative, the results can be expressed in numbers. There is nothing wrong with quantitative measures; they provide a useful overall picture. Quantitative studies, however, do not produce the rich source of information about customer satisfaction or expectations that are produced by "qualitative" studies.

An example of qualitative information is a collection of comments by customers who might respond to the invitation to fill in the blank lines on a comment card. The problem with qualitative data is that it becomes overwhelming and unwieldy when collected in large quantities.

It is very difficult to make actionable summary interpretations of qualitative feedback. These difficulties with qualitative data create a quandary. Either middle managers *summarize* the qualitive data to make it easier for senior managers to interpret, or they present top management with mountains of seemingly disorganized raw data. Two wonderful things happen when top officials take a direct interest in working with the "raw" qualitative data. First, they ensure that they don't become insulated and out of touch. Second, they give a powerful message to employees that it is important to satisfy each customer.

It's likely that the customer feedback you have currently is not specific enough to be useful. Almost certainly this feedback isn't available to the non-management employees and people on the front line.

To drive agency change using continuous improvement, you'll most likely need an entirely different kind of customer feedback—feedback that is useful to the individual or small team will give front-line people what they need to improve the most important part of their jobs: quality output, or customer satisfaction, or both. The kind of data that is most useful to front line teams tends to be small volume, qualitative feedback. I recommend that you reorganize your customer satisfaction research to collect mostly qualitative customer feedback, with just enough quantitative data to take a baseline and track progress.

When you use quantitative methods, the customer will typically be forced to answer the questions that you choose, using the answers that you make available in the boxes to check off. This can work if you know what questions to ask and include all of the possible answers for customers to choose from. In reality, researchers seldom ask the most interesting questions or put boxes in for every interesting answer the customer may want to give you.

What the customer thinks

Far more useful to the teams seeking to improve service quality is discovering what the customer thinks, wants, expects, or feels. If you want to know what the customer thinks is important, put in some blank lines for the customer to write on, or indicate a person for the customer to talk to. Without these measures you won't be able to predict all of the possible answers.

Experience	Customer	Grade
Knocks Their Socks Off	Dazzled	A
Exceeds Expectations	Pleased or Happy	B
As Expected	Satisfied	C
Fails, Customer Not Dependent	Irritated or Angry	D
Fails, Customer Dependent	Outraged	F

C U S T O M E R   S A T I S F A C T I O N

© 1991 Kaset International

There is another small problem with gathering customers' expectations from quantitative studies. If you ask customers to tell you what factors will make them satisfied with your services, they'll tell you. They will list a bunch of factors, and they'll even weight them for you so you know the relative importance of each factor. The problem is, customers consistently demonstrate that they "don't know" what *would* make them satisfied. So we have to choose between believing what customers predict would make them satisfied, and what they report actually made them feel satisfied.

I suggest that you put more weight in what customers report than what they predict; give more credit to their actions than to their words. From working with customers from a range of agencies, I recommend that you study satisfaction by asking customers to tell you why they are satisfied with your agency or with some other agency. When they demonstrate dissatisfaction by becoming irritated or angry, I suggest you find out why. I suggest you use the "critical incident" method of collecting customer feedback regarding satisfaction and loyalty.

The critical incident

Critical incident analysis is highly recommended for studying loyalty or satisfaction. The critical incident methodology is a "qualitative" process, which yields stories or comments, rather than neat, easily scored check-marks in boxes.

The questioner gathering customer satisfaction feedback for your agency would talk to customers, either over the phone or at your place of customer contact. The most useful level of detail is the "transaction," (or as Jan Carlson, CEO of SAS Airlines, coined it) the "moment of truth" in a service agency. To drive service or quality improvement, you want your customer feedback to be specific to the "moment of truth" or service attribute an action team will be assigned to improve.

As you learn to collect critical-incident feedback, it is important to seek feedback specifically about the transaction that you are seeking to improve.

Critical incidents provide feedback on expectations. You'll collect stories that illustrate why a customer is *very* satisfied or *very* dissatisfied. Merely being satisfied doesn't produce critical incident stories, and isn't even noticeable by the customer. Extremes in satisfaction (i.e., disappointment or surprise) yield the stories that offer you the richest feedback.

If a customer reports an incident that dissatisfied him, the story will frequently point out what the customer expected and how the agency failed to meet it. When a customer reports an incident that impressed him, he will frequently report that he didn't expect what he got and was happily surprised by it.

Critical incidents will illustrate the service elements that had an important impact on the customer's feelings. If the customer reports being impressed, then it becomes clear which actions or service elements have an important impact on customer satisfaction. Conversely, when a customer reports strong dissatisfaction, the critical incident that the customer describes reveals which service elements strongly affect the customer's feelings about the agency.

Constant feedback

In contrast to global studies, which tend to be annual or biannual, the feedback about transactions that your action teams need is continual, so it can be used for baselining, tracking improvement, and monitoring success.

First, your team needs to know the existing satisfaction level so they can use it as a baseline. Then, as they make changes in the way the moment of truth is managed or in the service element, they need to gather more feedback, so they can see the effects of the changes they are making. When they drive the satisfaction level up to the desired high level, they can stop improving it, and begin to simply monitor satisfaction to ensure that it stays high. After a moment of truth or a service element has been improved, the customer feedback needn't be continual, but it still needs to be collected regularly to ensure the changes are still in place and working.

If your change effort is truly ambitious, your agency needs to learn how to continually gather customer feedback—until the end of time, or as long as your agency aspires to high levels of quality or service. So, you might as well learn how to do it.

It doesn't require people with degrees in market research or statistics, just people who are willing to talk to customers and listen to their stories. It also requires caring enough to sort through the stories to find out what actually satisfies or dissatisfies customers.

You'll also discover that the act of surveying the customer, by itself, is an important "moment of truth." Most customers interpret a phone call or survey following a transaction as a demonstration of "caring" about customer satisfaction. Thus, the survey process itself shapes the customer's perception about the quality of your products or service. To get such a call from a government agency would likely be a memorable experience for any customer.

Chapter Nine

Not just another program

To reduce or eliminate the negative effects of bureaucracy, you'll need the help and support of the employees who are not in management.

If an agency has an alienated work group, or a lack of trust between employees and management, the agency may have to use outsiders to reach their employees.

The employees will need to understand that mission-driven is different than bureaucracy. They need to know that the existing ground rules won't work in the new model.

What follows in this chapter is the content of the message that needs to be delivered to employees in bureaucratic agencies that decide to make a serious commitment to becoming customer focused. I have included it here so that agencies planning to communicate the message themselves will understand the message that needs to be delivered. If you bring in outsiders to reach your people, you can use this chapter as an outline of the kind of message you want your suppliers to deliver.

Agencies that have a good level of trust between management and non-management can use this book as way of stimulating dialog, and building an organizational team.

What your employees need to understand in order to have your agency come together as one team with a new mission

When management asks front-line people to participate in something as all-encompassing as a new vision, or getting rid of bureaucracy, the first response is often fear. That fear is natural and understandable. To get beyond the fear takes understanding and acceptance of a new way of working.

This isn't just another "program." It isn't aimed at getting more work for fewer bucks. It isn't another step in the labor/management war. In essence, you're saying, "If you and your fellow employees join in the commitment to a customer or quality focus with the goal of eliminating bureaucracy, the labor/management war is over!"

Successful private-sector organizations are not at war with themselves. They are one team, in harmony, with a quality focus and a long-term view. The concept holds true for agencies of government as well. For your agency to thrive, all sides need to put away their parochial views and disarm. What's needed is one team, with one vision.

- The labor/management fight is over.
- The line/staff fight is over.
- The headquarters/field fight is over.

The appointed officials/civil servants fight is over. Anybody, whether labor, manager, professional, staff, or administration, who continues to act as though at war with some other part of the agency is standing in the way of your agency achieving its mission. Sure, you'll need some time to adjust. You'll need time to give up obsolete ways of thinking, and to adopt the new model.

If you are personally steeped in the old ways of internal strife and warfare, you need to change or get out. Otherwise, you'll hurt your agency, and that is not what they're paying you to do, or why you joined the agency in the first place.

Understanding the process, and your role in it

It's a new game, and hereafter, it is the customer, quality, or both, that count. Management has wised up to the realization that public satisfaction is a by-product of quality products or customer service. You don't achieve extraordinary quality and service by managing costs. You achieve extraordinary quality and service by managing quality and service.

If you think this is this year's program, you may well be mistaken. The intention is for a lifetime change. The objective is a permanent, agency-wide shift in the vision, the goal, and the culture.

- Stop watching the boss—watch the customer, the quality of your output, or both.

- Quit focusing on "your turf" or "your rights"—it's not an internal war any more. Focus on what you are contributing to the quality of your unit's output or satisfying the customer.

- You'll have a new union—a union of all the people in your agency coming together as one team.

If you're not serving the customer, you are probably serving someone who is. If your job is to serve someone within the agency, then your new challenge is to give your internal customers the same extraordinary service your agency wants to give to external customers.

In a service economy, we take turns serving each other. When it is our turn to serve, we give the customer the deference, the respect, and the dignity that customers deserve. When it's our turn to be served, we can then expect, and even demand, the deference, respect, and dignity we deserve.

Give the people you're directly serving the things they want from a service provider. Like customers everywhere, they want friendly and caring service, they want you to be flexible, they want you to help them resolve problems, and they want you to recover when you make a mistake or the agency goofs. That means:

1. Be friendly and caring.
2. Be flexible—stretch for the customer. Focus on the outcome, not the process.
3. Help your customer resolve problems.
4. Recover when your unit or the agency goofs
   a. Admit it when there has been a mistake
   b. Apologize on behalf of yourself, the work unit, or the agency
   c. Make it right, if you can
   d. Go the extra step: provide a symbolic atonement
   e. Follow up to be sure that customer satisfaction is "recovered."

No one changes overnight

The agency and the people in it can't and won't change overnight; we're all human. If you and your fellow workers take this new commitment seriously (and we don't incur any major foul-ups during the transition), it will still take years before you're where you want to be.

I've been observing some good people in good agencies making this transition, and it never goes as fast as you'd like. Still, the act of actually starting initiates a momentum that grows and grows until it has an energy of its own that pulls one along.

It isn't management alone who has to change; bureaucracy "contaminates" everyone in an agency. You find yourself waiting for someone to tell you what to do when you need to be taking your own initiatives. You find yourself afraid to act when you need to act for fear of being wrong.

To break away, you need to have the courage of your convictions. You'll find that bureaucracy has taken a lot away, and you'll need to take conscious steps if you want to pull your weight toward achieving the mission.

- Part of your job will be to get comfortable with responsibility and to take risks if you need to.

- Part of your job will be to get comfortable with the idea of pro-activity and initiative. In a bureaucracy, people didn't ask you to take initiatives and often made life difficult for you if you did.

- In a mission-driven agency, you'll need to step up to a situation if quality or customer satisfaction are threatened.

Cynics don't help. Blamers don't help. Complainers and whiners don't help. Help if you can. Get out if you can't help. And, if you can't help, or get out, at least keep quiet.

You'll be asked for feedback; give it straight, make it helpful

Even if you have a long history of being asked and never hearing anything back, open up and give feedback when it's requested. Sometime during the transition, you'll actually start getting some response back after you send it up the line.

- At some point, people are going to ask you, "How good is your boss at supporting you in your role?"

- You'll be asked to give feedback to others on your team and your peers, so that they can learn to be good team players.

The idea is to change the feedback system so that it doesn't all come down from the top. Eventually, you'll be getting feedback from those you serve, from your peers and from your manager. The feedback will be less painful because it won't be coming from the perspective of monitoring, controlling, and disciplining that marked the bureaucratic system. Instead, the feedback will be more from the perspective of coaching, so you can become a more valuable member of the team.

If you serve internal or external customers, you'll be asked what your customers say they want from you or your work unit. It's now well understood that people who serve customers are a good proxy for the customers themselves. So, you'll be asked for your ideas on what the agency can do to support you in satisfying your customers.

You'll be asked, "What policies, practices, and procedures stand in the way of your achieving quality outputs or serving your customers well?" Departments that serve you will be asking you, "How well are you being served by the people, policies, practices and procedures of the work units that serve you?" Don't hurt, but don't hold back. Be straight, say what you think and feel, so people can learn what it will take to give you extraordinary service. Don't make them guess.

You'll be asked, "What suggestions can you make that will improve the products or services that you are providing your customers?" Perhaps for the first time, the agency will be receptive to suggestions and ideas.

The bureaucratic defensiveness, insulation from customer feedback and turf protection that squelched so many good ideas in the past will gradually disappear.

Chapter Ten

Challenging basic beliefs

You'll need to challenge some beliefs that may be basic to your culture.

Here is a list of beliefs that will need to be gradually changed as your culture adapts to the a mission-driven model.

It is bureaucratic to believe that "all functions and people need to be under control"

To become mission-driven, it is valuable to give up the idea of control, and believe in the value of responsiveness, or flexibility. Customer satisfaction can't be controlled. You do your best to earn it, but you can't demand it or control it. Control focuses on processes. Customer and quality visions focus on "outcomes."

To achieve service quality, it is useful to give up the managerial compulsion to control, or be in control, and trust that if the agency is aligned around the vision, and is flexible and responsive enough to achieve the vision, the agency will achieve more than you alone could, striving for the sense of being in "control." In a customer-focused agency managers are more like supporters, coaches, and obstacle removers.

It is bureaucratic to think that all functions of planning and control have to be done by management

To be customer focused or to achieve total quality, much of the planning, controlling, reacting, responding, and flexing needs to be done by front-line people—by people who don't manage others, but instead manage the achievement of quality or the satisfaction of customers.

It is bureaucratic to believe that work should be divided by functional specialty

One of the principles of the bureaucratic model is that work be divided by functional specialties, and where possible, done by specialists. The result of this belief is that workers tend to be organized into groups of people who do similar work, rather than into groups of people who do different work, yet combine talent to provide everything needed to serve the customer. Organizing employees by specialty this way hinders the attainment of quality products or satisfied customers.

Agencies seeking total quality or customer satisfaction will organize people by outcomes desired, products produced, or customers served. This ensures that a commitment to quality or service drives the work unit, rather than their commitment to a craft or specialty. The agency still maintains people with the needed special skills, but the specialists aren't grouped along with others having the same skill. They are grouped into multi-disciplinary teams that accomplish great things in an atmosphere of enthusiasm.

It is bureaucratic to manage with a "problem-solving" approach

In the problem-solving approach, someone (usually a manager) looks at a problem, "fixes" that problem, then moves on to the next problem with no encouragement to address the root cause.

When quality or customer satisfaction is everyone's goal, then problems need not be solved by managers alone. Empowered people, aspiring to continuous improvement, can be trained to not only solve the immediate problem, but also to find the root causes and fix them.

It is bureaucratic to think that managers and managing are more important than the people who achieve the quality or satisfy individual customers

Those who strive to become customer focused, or to achieve total quality, soon discover that the truly "important" people are the ones who are part of achieving the total quality or who satisfy the customers. Regardless of what management wants, says, or does, if the front-line people aren't making it happen, the mission isn't achieved.

Team members need to know that the management doesn't rank people in terms of importance. Every job and every role is important. It's important to realize that being higher up on the organizational chart does not mean you are more important that others. Eventually, managers' need to feel more important becomes much less of an issue.

It seems to be a basic precept of bureaucracy that ambiguity is intolerable, and needs to be resolved

In bureaucracy, things need to be black or white. There is no room for gray. To achieve total quality or to consistently satisfy customers, your agency and your people need to have some tolerance for ambiguity.

In the real world, there is a lot of gray. If you attempt to make things black or white, you miss too much. Rules can be unambiguous, while guidelines are ambiguous, e.g., "If the guidelines don't work to achieve the mission, then forget the guidelines and do what it takes achieve the mission." That's pretty gray.

It is bureaucratic to think that consistency has value

This is most widely held and perhaps the most damaging belief underlying bureaucracy. Perhaps at one time consistency was seen as an aid to good quality, or to satisfying customers, but, as the focus of the agency turns inward, the idea becomes simply that consistency is important.

Consistency certainly is important in producing components that make up a product. In the absence of good reason for changing, consistency has value in relationships. Consistency in choices or decisions, however, can sometimes be a barrier to good quality, or to satisfying customers. Much of the damage to quality or to customer satisfaction comes from the excessive concern that bureaucracies attach to the idea of consistency without regard for the outcomes produced.

For those striving for quality or customer satisfaction, it is okay to view consistency as nice and comfortable as long as it helps achieves the desired quality or results in satisfied customers. The moment that it gets in the way of quality or customer satisfaction, forget consistency and substitute flexibility.

It is bureaucratic to believe that more choices for the customer will confuse them

Bureaucracies prefer to believe that more choices for customers and employees and will be confusing for them. The reality is that choices are confusing to those making up the rules. To keep their jobs simple, rule makers tend to minimize the number of choices given to customers and employees. One might say, "The more bureaucratic the agency, the fewer choices offered to customers and employees."

Agencies that empower their employees to make decisions aimed at satisfying customers find that the employees will create lots of choices for customers because customers like to be satisfied. The more choices there are, the more likely it is the customer will find one that satisfies.

It is bureaucratic to believe that equal treatment for everybody is fair for all

This notion is closely related to the idea of consistency. All you can say about equal treatment for all is that it will result in unequal satisfaction for all. Bureaucracies value the process of equal treatment, but ignore the outcome of unequal satisfaction.

If you strive for an objective outcome, like quality in your product, or customer satisfaction from your service, then you will find it useful to confront the misperception that equal treatment for all is good. You will instead substitute belief in the idea that equal satisfaction for all customers is a much fairer goal than equal treatment for all.

How do you want to be measured? By the *treatment* you give, or by the *outcome* you achieve? Customers are only interested in satisfaction. If equal treatment doesn't satisfy them, then they expect you to treat them unequally.

If you leap to the conclusion that unequal treatment is unjust, then consider the benefits of offering choices. Giving the customer lots of choices makes it possible to provide as many different treatments as customers tell you they need in order to be satisfied.

Until recently, the Florida Department of Motor Vehicles treated everybody the same. To get a license, you went to the office and stood in line. They didn't offer appointments. By treating everybody the same, they made some people dissatisfied.

Then they began offering appointments. The customer can call up for an appointment in advance, or, if the customer prefers not to wait for an appointment, or needs something today, the customer still has the option to come anytime and wait in line. By offering a choice, the Department of Motor Vehicles increased the number of citizens who are satisfied with their service.

It is bureaucratic to believe if I do it for one, I have to do it for everyone

Another false belief that underlies bureaucracy is the notion of the slippery slope: "If I do it for one, I have to do it for everybody." This argument pops up almost automatically in bureaucratic thinking, and is kin to the belief in consistency and equal treatment for all. This notion is pervasive because there are some situations in which it may be true.

The error is in over-generalizing the idea and applying it where it is patently false, and almost foolish. Agencies that value total quality, or customer focus, want their people to make decisions and choices based on the mission outcome, and not on the process. So, the process becomes much more flexible, as long as it is aimed at achieving the desired outcome.

The Federal Emergency Management Administration has been hand-cuffed by procedures that require the Agency to obtain a written request from the governor before delivering assistance in a state in which disaster has struck. When Hurricane Andrew devastated large parts of Florida last year, as any television viewer could immediately see, the state needed help—and quickly. In the future, perhaps, the FEMA personnel will be empowered to respond quickly in exceptional cases, without upsetting standard operating procedure.

You have to trust that most people are reasonable and understanding, and realize that adapting the process to satisfy one customer doesn't mean that you will have to make that same accommodation to all customers.

Chapter Eleven

The shadow organization strategy

A shadow organization is an informal organization, superimposed upon a formal organization. If you are used to terms like "steering committee," or "task force," or "action teams," then you are most likely using some form of shadow organization now.

Agencies form "shadow" organizations to get work done that is difficult to do within the formal agency. Other terms the mean the same thing are "informal" organizations, or "parallel" organizations.

This chapter will provide a brief overview on using a shadow organization as a way of implementing change within a bureaucracy.

There are many benefits of installing a shadow organization. Managers in bureaucratic agencies tend to be busy, and often can't find the time to drive organizational change. They can, however, monitor the change process. The use of a shadow organization allows managers to *monitor* as opposed to *do*.

- The shadow organization can have a flat hierarchy, and can empower people to make decisions based on skills and experience rather than agency level. The teams can be cross functional so they can cut through the departmental boundary walls that bureaucratic agencies traditionally immobilize.

- The shadow organization can be sharply focused. Its mission is to change the way the agency functions.

- When driving a lot of change, the agency needs to be able to respond quickly. The shadow organization can do that, whereas the functional organization is slow to respond or adapt.

Profiling the shadow organization

A typical shadow organization for a service quality improvement effort might include:

The senior management group—Senior management decides on the goal and the scope of the effort, and creates the mandate. For example, continuous improvement of service quality.

A steering committee—The steering committee might be made up of some senior managers and some upper-middle managers, and their role would be to actually implement the continuous improvement effort. The steering committee would form the task forces and empower them and monitor their success until the desired goal state is achieved.

Task forces—Task forces would be made up of cross functional teams of middle-managers and professional staff who would define and monitor the action teams that would actually do the work of continually improving service quality. Task forces will support the action teams with responsive approvals, assignments, and links to the agency so that the shadow organization and functional organization work smoothly together.

Action teams—The action teams will be made up of front-line people who will actually implement continuous improvement of service quality. The action teams will apply proven problem-solving strategies to fix both internal and external customer problems, and add service enhancements to provide exceptional service to internal and external customers.

Managers throughout all of the units in the functional organization will be assigned to participate in task forces in the shadow organization. Their purpose will be to ensure that the two agencies stay aligned.

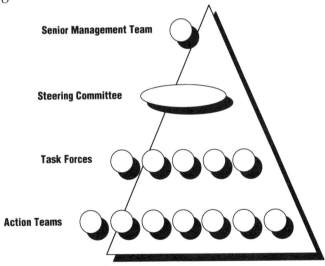

The chart above is an example of how a shadow organization might be organized. The chart illustrates a senior management team, one steering committee, six task forces, and a number of action teams. There is no standard form that a shadow organization has to take, however, and each agency will decide to structure its shadow organization the way that best suits the particular situation and culture.

If the idea of a "shadow organization" is new to you, imagine a traditional agency. It is managed by hierarchy with each level controlling those levels below it and being controlled by the levels above. Now, if we took a group of middle managers from the various functional units in the traditional agency and assigned them roles in a task force, we are creating a second agency on top of the base agency.

When the people in the task force are doing their regular jobs, their reporting relationships are clear and their level of authority is also clear. When those same people are acting in their secondary roles, as members of the task force, they could have different reporting relationships and might have different levels of authority.

Suppose ABC Agency is organized in functional units in the traditional manner. The head of the agency becomes concerned about employee morale, however, an issue that need work across multiple departments. So, she ap-
points a task force
to work on em-
ployee morale and
calls it the "morale
task force." She
names someone
leader of the task
force, and asks the
leader to report to
the agency head
on the activities of
the task force.

In this example, we have a shadow organization being formed out of, and superimposed upon, the existing agency. The task force leader now has two reporting relationships. During normal situations, the leader reports to an associate administrator. On the activities of the morale task force, the leader reports to the agency head. Each of the members of the task force normally reports to different managers, and now each of them also reports to the leader of the task force for activities relating to the morale task force.

Name that unit

In the example above, we call the morale task force a "cross-functional" task force because it brings people together from a variety of functional units. If the head of the agency had picked the team from all the people in one field office, we would call the team a "natural work unit" task force.

Multi-disciplinary teams can be either from one functional unit or from several functional units.

A management information systems department might have several sections organized by discipline: the programming section, the operators' section, the systems section, the data base section, etc. If the MIS department formed a task force with a member from each section, that team could be called multi-disciplinary, even though it represents only one function within the agency—MIS.

Tackling what doesn't get tackled

Task forces are set up, they do a job, and then they disappear. A task force, by its nature, is elastic, flexible, changeable, and ethereal. Task forces can be formed easily and can disappear just as easily. The charter of the task force can be changed, modified, flexed, or even totally eliminated.

The dynamics of any bureaucratic agency, however, result in resistance to significant changes. Small changes are allowed and accepted as normal, but significant or meaningful changes are resisted. A change in mission is such a significant change that the · bureaucratic agency probably couldn't achieve it without some help.

The effect of the shadow organization is to work around the stabilizing force of the functional units in stasis and introduce changes that the functional organization is better able to accept.

When an agency undertakes to make a significant change—either in its mission, vision, or strategy—it is sometimes necessary to form a large number of shadow units, which all work together to achieve the change. Suppose that the incoming Secretary of a Cabinet level agency is committed to changing the agency's basic mission, vision, and strategy, and create a customer-focused agency, with a customer-focused mission, vision, and strategy. This kind of change is too much for one task force. The following units might be formed to work on this change:

- A senior management team
- A steering committee to manage the transition
- Six task forces to link with the existing functional units
- Several dozen action teams, to manage various assignments during the transition.

When you introduce more than a few shadow units and link them you are essentially creating an entire second level of organization, superimposed upon the existing functional organization.

Purpose of the shadow organization

The purpose of the shadow organization within any given agency depends on the goal that executive management wants to achieve. The design of the shadow organization also depends on the goal you choose.

Let's examine three possible goal states that an agency might choose. I've arbitrarily assigned these names that are sometimes used interchangeably: "customer sensitive," "customer focused," and "customer driven," but each of them have specific meanings here.

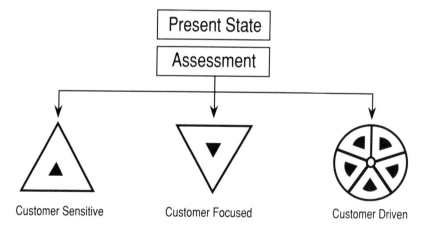

A "customer-sensitive" agency

An agency choosing the goal state seeks to maintain its existing organizational form while improving service quality. Given the goal of maintaining the existing agency, the shadow organization's purpose will be to come into existence, improve service quality, and then disappear.

Given the desire to maintain the existing agency, and use the shadow organization as a method for achieving change, it makes sense to make all shadow organization roles temporary. One way to do this is to consider these assignments as temporary, and rotate people through the shadow organization and then back to a job in the functional organization, or to make all of the assignments part-time.

Given the goal of maintaining the existing agency while bringing service quality up to customer expectations, the duration of the shadow organization may be fairly short.

The shadow organization could disappear in a variety of scenarios. The best scenario would be that service quality goals are achieved and the shadow organization is dismantled thoughtfully. Less promising scenarios could see the end of the shadow organization because of any of the following reasons:

- An unexpected budget crunch
- A change in senior management, e.g., a new Secretary
- Tension between the shadow and functional organizations
- Shadow organization people stressed by handling two jobs
- New issues superseding service quality improvement
- Outside influences (Congress or the President) changing priorities

At the Environmental Protection Agency, a shadow organization was formed to overhaul procurement policies and their relationships with contractors. The existing organization, which was thought to have led to the problem, couldn't be counted upon to change itself. Once the needed changes were accomplished the shadow organization disbanded.

A "customer-focused" agency

An agency choosing this goal state adopts a *customer-focused* mission, but otherwise maintains the bureaucratic organizing form. This goal state is chosen by agencies seeking extraordinary service quality.

The purpose of the shadow organization will be to co-exist permanently with the functional organization. The shadow organization will gradually take over all customer contact or product quality responsibility. The challenge is to make sure that the functional organization does not get in the way of the customer-focused mission.

The inclination of the functional part of the agency will be to set up barriers to customer satisfaction through its in-focused goals and activities. On the other hand, the shadow organization must take care that it doesn't "flaunt" its new culture, values, or mission as superior to that of the functional organization.

Given the goal of converting to a customer-focused mission while maintaining the rest of the existing agency, it makes sense to make some of the steering committee and task force assignments full-time, permanent jobs, and to staff the shadow organization with "fast track" management talent who have the potential to become senior management within the functional organization.

The use of action teams (made up of non-management people) will probably be a permanent change in the way that the functional organization operates. Hence it makes sense to use functional supervisors in new roles as facilitators and coaches of the action teams. This will encourage supervisors to coach rather than discipline.

To achieve its goals, the shadow organization will differ from the functional organization in many ways, evolving away from rigid hierarchy, and using empowerment as the norm.

Rules will be relaxed somewhat and become guidelines that are put aside when they interfere with the mission. The human component of interpersonal relations will be added in both internal and external customer transactions. The shadow organization will have as much cross-functional and multi-disciplinary teaming as needed to overcome the bureaucratic barriers that exist within the functional organization.

As the shadow organization strengthens and produces successes, the tension between it and the functional organization itself will build. This tension can be managed and competitiveness can be reduced with planning, training, and understanding. The more the two become aligned around the customer-focused mission, the less conflict will be produced.

Such a situation can be seen at the Office of Personal Management (OPM) and the Federal Quality Institute. The Institute, which started out as a temporary agency, has become institutionalized over time to keep constant pressure on and to offer support for quality efforts in the federal government. Both agencies now exist without friction; both have their specific areas of focus.

A "customer-driven" agency

An agency choosing this customer-driven goal state adopts whatever organizational form is needed to achieve extraordinary customer relations. The goal here is to install a new culture and a new way of organizing, managing, and operating that is totally customer driven. In this case, the existing functional organization will not permanently co-exist with the shadow organization; through the shadow organization, it will gradually be transformed into a new organization and the traditional functional organization will disappear.

The shadow organization needs to be selected most carefully. In this situation, your very best people are needed to create the shadow organization, and to build the shadow organization to such a level of strength, talent, and commitment that it will stand as a skeleton onto which the remainder of the functional organization gradually can be built.

The shadow organization will be made up largely of permanent assignments (at least at the steering committee and task force level). The shadow organization will become the training ground and development base for the future agency. Everything that the people who populate the shadow organization learn will be valuable skills in the transformed agency. In most ways, the transformed agency will have attributes identical to those of the units in the shadow organization.

Shadow organization cultures may vary

Depending upon the goal state, the desired culture in the shadow organization will vary. If the goal is to be a customer-sensitive agency, then the culture of the shadow organization will largely reflect that of the functional organization. One exception will be in the expected cooperation and collaboration between team members. It might be accepted behavior in the functional organization for people in different units to be uncooperative and even competitive, the behavior of people in the shadow organization, however, will need to be collaborative.

In situations where the goal state is customer focused or customer driven, it is important to purposely manage the culture of the shadow organization. The culture can be managed by a task force, the steering committee, or through the training of all members of the shadow organization.

Regardless of the goal state, the shadow organization needs to have responsive standards far different from the underlying functional organization. For example, in one organization that functioned so slowly its people described it as "glacial," requests from action teams to task forces required responses within 72 hours. If no response was received within 72 hours, the action team could consider their recommendation or request approved.

The culture of the shadow organization needs to be less hierarchical and more attuned to empowerment; less concerned with rules and more with the mission; less concerned with process and more concerned with outcomes; more human, personal, and concerned more with individual needs and less with the formal application of procedures or policies.

The functional organization

The functional organization is, of course, the original organization from which the shadow organization was drawn. The role of the functional organization is to conduct business as usual while the shadow organization is interacting with it to gradually improve service quality.

Periodically, the functional organization will receive feedback from the communications task force, from the steering committee, and from senior management about the efforts to improve service quality. It will also receive regular requests for cooperation with the shadow organization as existing work processes are changed to improve customer satisfaction.

When employing a shadow organization (depending on the desired goal state), people within the functional organization will be preparing either for a return to business as usual sometime in the future, or the permanent establishment of the shadow organization, or the eventual transition to a new organizational form.

Chapter Twelve

A new vision for education

What would happen if we were to apply the principles in this book to public education?

To give you a vivid example of how a mission-driven organizing form would work, I've chosen the field of education, about which everyone has opinions. I will share with you my vision for how the educational system might be changed to focus directly on the needs of the customers. I chose education because of the involvement of government at the federal, state, and local levels.

What you are about to read may be so foreign to you that your initial reaction may be anything from bewilderment, or rejection, to glee. The examples for dispensing education-related services don't "fit" any contemporary government service delivery system.

Here then is a "vision" of how public education might look if we applied the principles of debureaucratization—replacing bureaucracy with a customer-focused, mission-driven approach to education.

Dispensing services in public education

I was asked to contribute to a vision for public education by a collaborative alliance of public- and private-sector agencies seeking to restructure education in the State of Florida. The quest to make the educational system "customer focused" led to the conclusion that the student—or when the student is a minor, some combination of student/parent—is the "customer."

What students want in a learning experience

Once it is clear that the student is the customer, then the way to attract them to education is to determine what students want out of a learning experience. Here are a basic set of assumptions about what students want, drawn from formal and informal surveys of students and former students.

- Students want a choice about what they learn.
- They want a feeling of having some control.
- Students also want to learn at a rate that is right for them— their own rate. Virtually all students want the rate to be challenging enough so learning isn't boring, and yet not so

challenging that it produces frustration. The delicacy of this balance dictates that the student needs to be the one that controls the learning rate.

- Students want to experience desirable feelings during the learning experience. The learning could be *interesting* (satisfying curiosity), or it could be *fun* (exciting, stimulating, challenging, rewarding). The learning could be *inspiring* (creates models, shows that obstacles can be overcome, illustrates loving nurturance), or it could be *dramatic* (capturing interest through dramatic tension and ultimate resolution). Or, the learning might *promise a desirable reward* (driver's training, sports, homemaking, career training, enhanced attractiveness, increased social acceptance).

- Students prefer to set and *achieve* their learning goals. They want the freedom to set low or high goals, and they want to be free to change from one mode to another. They are willing to reduce their goals, or take longer than planned, but they want to succeed, not fail.

To summarize: to be customer focused, learning needs to be:

- student-paced
- individualized
- interesting, stimulating, challenging, inspirational, dramatic, promising, or fun
- assured of success, and free of failure
- with the degree of challenge and effort demanded being changeable and always determined by the student

Careful analysis of the list above leads to the conclusion that "customer-driven" education needs to be individualized, self-paced, carefully and artfully crafted, and available when the student wants it.

To succeed in satisfying our customer then, we either need to make a world-class teacher available on demand for one-on-one tutoring for each child, OR, we have to make heavy use of futuristic computer-aided interactive learning systems.

Visit to a new paradigm school

Since the student will play such an important role in the new paradigm, it is fitting to view the new paradigm first from the viewpoint of the students. Imagine that the steps proposed by the collaborative alliance for school restructuring have been realized, and we are able to visit a "new paradigm" school 20 years from now.

As with any school today, the school of the future will engage the student in a combination of activities that alternate between quiet sessions of reading, studying, listening, and socializing sessions where students speak, react, question, practice, and demonstrate what they have learned. Let's begin by observing students during the "quiet" sessions of the future.

The "silent" cubicles

We begin our tour by observing Mrs. Swanson's class, a typical room full of students engaged in learning. The students in this room represent ages ranging from the elderly, with a scattering of adults, some teenagers, and some younger children. Each student has a "silent" cubicle (booth or module). Each student may be speaking, or listening, even singing, or practicing an instrument, yet, electronic noise suppression is eradicating all surrounding sounds, so that no student hears any sounds made by others.

Each cubicle contains a computer, a monitor (high-resolution digital television screen), with several input devices. The student can use the keyboard, a note pad that reads handwritten input, a microphone that accepts verbal input, a scanner that reads text and photos or drawings, a mouse, a joystick, and gloves that allow the computer to sense complete hand movements. All of this equipment has been installed by private-sector computer companies on a "pay-for-performance" plan under which the competitive computer suppliers keep the equipment at a "state-of-the-art" level and accept the risk of technological obsolescence.

Customer-focused education: helping immigrants to adjust

The first student we observe is Juan, a new enrollee whose family recently immigrated to our town from a small town in Argentina where the new paradigm schools have not yet arrived.

Juan is getting acquainted with the new paradigm learning system. The system and Juan are having a conversation in Juan's native language. The computer is determining Juan's present level of reading speed, comprehension, and vocabulary. In addition to language skills, the computer is assessing Juan's ability to deal with numbers, and other assorted skills.

The computer asks Juan to listen to several different "accent" modules to see which accent of Spanish Juan finds most understandable when spoken by the computer. None of the accent modules are exactly right for Juan, but he finds one that he feels is closest to Spanish as it is spoken in his part of Argentina.

The computer is "making friends" with Juan. The goal is to teach Juan how to use the computer, and to teach the computer a great deal about Juan. In answer to queries, the computer determines that Juan's deepest concerns are about making friends in this new school, and about his ability to learn in spite of his limited knowledge of English.

The computer assures Juan that he will be able to learn in both his own language and English. The computer explains that it will use Spanish for his initial instruction and gradually teach Juan English. The computer will be able to keep track of Juan's progress in English and will make the transition to English as quickly as Juan is ready.

The computer also has asked a number of personal questions about Juan, his interests, his goals, his concerns, his beliefs, and what he looks for in friends. The computer selects the closest match it can find from a file of volunteers, and assigns another student to be Juan's initial mentor.

Whichever input medium Juan chooses to use, the computer will gradually refine Juan's input so there will be continual and gradual improvement. When Juan uses the slate for handwritten inputs, he will discover that over time, his handwriting gets better and better as he is gently forced to write with better and better handwriting so the computer will be able to understand him.

As Juan learns keyboard skills, the computer will patiently coach him to gradually develop speed and accuracy. As Juan uses voice input, the computer will gradually and patiently give Juan feedback about his clarity and articulation and grammar. Juan will, almost without being aware of it, gradually develop good verbal skills in both Spanish and English.

Juan's mother also registers

Juan's mother, Mrs. Gomez, is delighted to learn that she can enroll Juan immediately. The school operates year round, and students may start at any time, without waiting for the beginning of a semester. Juan has chosen his mother as his "coach," and it is as Juan's coach, rather than as a student, that Mrs. Gomez signs in to the computer.

The computer "makes friends" with Juan's mother in much the same way that it made friends with Juan. She will learn how to operate the computer using whichever input devices she prefers, so she can communicate easily with the system.

Once the computer and Juan's mother can communicate with each other, the computer begins to teach Mrs. Gomez the role of "coach."

Mrs. Gomez learns the importance of her role of "coach," and how she can support her son to achieve his learning goals. She is given a variety of ways in which she can be helpful, and in cooperation with the computer, she agrees to a commitment with which she feels comfortable. Mrs. Gomez agrees to use the computer at least every two weeks for consultation on Juan's learning achievement and her role as coach.

Mrs. Gomez is pleased to find that she can consult the system after work, or before work, or, if the family gets its own home computer, she will be able to engage the system from home.

Mrs. Gomez instructs the computer regarding her beliefs about Juan's instruction in certain sensitive areas. She is raising Juan as a Catholic, but has no reservations about Juan learning about other religions (if he chooses) or about issues such as scientific creationism or evolution.

Mrs. Gomez does, however, have strong views about sex education, and wishes to reserve her son's sex education for her and her husband. The computer acknowledges her choice, and confirms that Juan will not be offered sex education at school.

The final issue on the agenda is Mrs. Gomez' concern that Juan might learn South American history from the perspective of the North Americans, and that he will have a distorted view of his native land. The computer assures Mrs. Gomez that Juan will receive special instruction about his native land, including history presented from an Argentinian perspective.

The computer points out that Juan will also receive instruction in the North American historical perspective, and assures Mrs. Gomez that Juan will be helped to create his own synthesis of the two views.

Customer-focused education: teaching basic and elective skills

In the next cubicle, Jimmy is playing an adventure game. Jimmy is somewhere in a medieval castle, striving to defeat a variety of enemies in order to rescue a Russian princess. The computer says, "You've come to an oak door, with no visible doorknob. What do you want to do"? Jimmy types in "Nock on it." The computer responds, "Do you mean **K**nock?"

As we watch Jimmy play the game, the computer is engaged in two activities at the same time. The computer is challenging Jimmy to solve the puzzle and rescue the princess, and at the same time, the computer is introducing new words in English, as well as Russian, which Jimmy has chosen to learn.

Next to Jimmy is Felicia, who is fascinated with languages. She is currently learning six languages and is at an advanced level of learning in all of them. The computer has told her that she could satisfy the language requirement for a work certificate in any of five languages, yet she keeps adding new capabilities. Felicia has no interest in math, nor does math play a role in her career goal. She wants to be an interpreter for the United Nations, and has determined that she will need only rudimentary math skills to achieve her career objectives.

In her "living skills" module, she demonstrated the mathematics skills necessary to be a capable consumer.

At her request, the computer has stopped introducing new math skills. The computer does reinforce her existing math skills by quizzing her in math problems in different languages. This has the purpose of extending Felicia's capabilities as a capable consumer into several additional cultures and languages other than her own, and it also serves to refresh and strengthen her basic skills.

Since she has elected to learn cultures and languages, the computer is teaching her the differences and similarities between the way her native government is organized and how other governments are organized. Felicia doesn't even notice that she is cementing an understanding of her own country's government as she learns how it compares to other systems of government.

Within the context of language instruction, Felicia is learning all of the other disciplines (math, science, history, social sciences) that were often taught separately in the old paradigm.

Customer-focused education: career guidance

Tom has chosen instruction in what he would need to know to be a successful professional athlete. Tom is too young to know whether he has the skills to become a professional—he simply has an interest in that career objective.

The computer will guide Tom's learning of the basic reading, writing, math, science, and core studies, in the context of what a professional athlete would need to know. His math training will take the form of calculating batting averages or quarterback ratings. His science will include why a curve ball curves, or why a golf ball travels further at higher altitudes.

Tom will be encouraged to "try out" many careers beyond sports before he leaves school for college or the work world. Each potential career will provide a new context for learning and a new demand for specific learning, which Tom may or may not choose to pursue. For example, the "pro athlete" module offers limited mathematics, and doesn't include trigonometry. If, however, Tom later chooses to "try out" being a surveyor, he will certainly learn trigonometry.

Cindy has been going through all of the "helping" professions. She has tried out being a nurse, being a doctor, being a parent, being a therapist, and now she is trying out being a teacher. The context of teacher will allow Cindy to use the skills she has developed in the other helping professions, and in addition teach Cindy some new skills related to helping others to learn.

As we observe, Cindy is interacting with a simulated student group. The simulated student group is made up of demanding and reactive students. As long as Cindy is interacting with the group, and using facilitative skills, the group reacts well. Any time that Cindy lapses into "teaching" mode, and lectures, the group reacts negatively.

The use of immediate and exaggerated feedback through simulation allows Cindy to get the input she needs to develop her ability to facilitate learning. The simulated sessions, paced by Cindy's learning rate, are used to build skills in the safety of the "silent" cubicle. They will be followed by a series of instructional opportunities, ranging from one-on-one tutoring for fellow students, to full group facilitations that she will conduct.

Customer-focused education: developing human relations skills

In certain team learning exercises, Leon's friends have given Leon constructive feedback about being a "team player."

The computer has suggested—and Leon agrees—that it would be useful to learn how to be more open to the opinions and suggestions of other people.

Leon has been following a series of learning goals aimed at being an engineer, and he has come to understand that effective engineers need team skills, and they need to be open to input from other people. Leon is presently learning these skills and to use group process to arrive at consensual solutions. The computer is simulating a group meeting. Computer-generated individuals appear on the screen and make their contributions toward solving a problem that is just beyond Leon's skills to solve. The group process will take place in "slow motion," so Leon can be aware of his "automatic" responses, as well as the new responses that he has chosen to substitute for the unproductive ones.

Once Leon is confident with his new skills, he will be called into a series of group process workshops where he will apply his new skills in a real life setting. He'll work with others who have completed the modules on group process, higher order thinking, or both.

Customer-focused education: pursuit of the arts

Ms. Barnard is retired and is studying music. She has loved music all of her life, but never had the time or opportunity to study it. She is exploring the classical literature and learning to understand the music she loves.

Ms. Barnard is listening to a Beethoven sonata. On her screen, she can watch a variety of images. She can watch the pianist playing the sonata in one corner of her screen. In another corner, she can watch the music as it is written in musical notation. In another corner, she can watch the musical notation with descriptive phrases flashing. An arrow flashes at a bar of music, and the description says, "beginning of second theme."

She is simultaneously observing performance; she is relating the music she hears to the notation she sees; she is learning the underlying structure that makes music "classical;" she is refining her ear as she has her listening attention directed to what she is hearing.

Ms. Barnard has many choices ahead of her as she learns more about the music she loves. She may choose to learn how to play an instrument. She may choose to learn how to conduct. She may choose to learn to compose. She may simply choose to shut off the instruction and listen to the classical literature she loves.

Customer-focused Education: expanding teaching skills

Mrs. Swanson is the teacher in support of this room full of "silent cubicles." Angela is having difficulty working through her reading. The computer keeps using words that are new to Angela. When Angela points to the word and asks the computer to define it, the computer patiently does so, but then reminds Angela that she already has learned the word, used it in context, spelled it, and that it has been part of her vocabulary for a long time.

Mrs. Swanson quickly discovers that the computer has mistaken Angela for a different student. She resets the computer so Angela can sign on and verify that the computer is using Angela's vocabulary and skill record, rather than one for another student. While Mrs. Swanson is working with Angela, she asks Angela to access any "help requests" that Angela has stored up for discussion with a teacher. Angela accesses her library and finds an item she'd like help with.

Angela is "trying out" being a writer, and the first item is a question that she noted while reading Shakespeare's *Romeo and Juliet*: "How can I find out more about family feuds, how they could be stopped, and why people continue them?" Mrs. Swanson quickly verifies that Angela is not asking her for that information, but wants to do a little exploring on this subject and seeks guidance or advice on how to approach her exploration.

Mrs. Swanson accesses the master "pathing" program (akin to an encyclopedia index), which maps all of the depths to which a student could explore the word "feud." Mrs. Swanson discusses the various options shown, and offers several suggestions for a path that might satisfy Angela's curiosity, yet not go far beyond what Angela is curious about.

Customer-focused education: developing entrepreneurial skills

Ralph lives in the heart of what once was called the "ghetto," and is an example of a youngster that once would have been considered "at risk." Ralph is learning to be a shopkeeper. He began with the introductory module that surveyed the skills and competencies of a good shopkeeper. Much of his primary education was given in the context of being a shopkeeper. He learned to read by practicing reading labels on clothing, invoices, or advertisements. He learned his math by pricing stock, calculating mark ups, calculating discounts, and determining percentages of profit on revenues. Ralph has progressed through the modules that offer insight and understanding into the complexities of inventories, bookkeeping, customer satisfaction, and managing shop employees. Ralph has now reached the level of application for the skills he has learned, and is deeply involved with a computer simulation of running a grocery market. He orders stock, balances his cash, and coaches and encourages simulated store employees. He moves easily between the "street" dialect and the "television" dialect in English, and he has built a limited facility with Spanish and Korean, the other common languages of his neighborhood.

Ralph practices good customer skills in dialogues with a variety of simulated customers. He speaks to the customers in their preferred language, and understands enough of what the customers are saying to him to conduct business.

As we observe, we can see how motivated and energized Ralph is by the opportunity to apply his skills toward his goal. Ralph is clear about his goals, his values, his commitment to his community, and is making instructional choices that are right for Ralph. With a supportive coach, we can be confident that Ralph will have the skills to achieve his dream.

In the next silent cubicle, Mr. Hubert is learning a new career skill. He had been an industrial worker, but he injured his back. He has come to school to find a new marketable skill. While he was working, he observed people doing accounting work in his company. He thought he might like to do that kind of work.

Mr. Hubert selected the same learning module that is used by students "trying out" being an accountant. After a survey of the skills needed, and a little practice at the kind of work accountants do, Mr. Hubert reaffirmed his choice. The computer supported him, and he has been learning the skills necessary to get his competency certificate in accounting.

Customer-focused education: life skills

Lori is "trying out" being a wife and mother. All of her current instruction is within the context of those roles. She has completed a module designed to examine her expectations and realign them more with reality than with family life as shown in movies.

She is presently working on strategies for coping with things in her situation that she can't control or change. The pretest for the coping module tells the computer module where to put its emphasis. Lori is discovering that she relies heavily on a single strategy for coping with upsetting situations. She is becoming aware that she uses "avoidance" as her primary coping strategy, and the module is helping her to discover and learn to practice a wider range of coping skills, such as negotiation and choosing acceptance.

The life skills series aims at giving individuals a balanced set of behaviors, so they can choose those strategies most likely to produce the outcomes they seek. As with all other contextual learning, life skills are one medium through which the individual is open to instruction in verbal and written communication, math, the sciences, history, the arts, and other fields of human learning. As she progresses in her skills, the computer will match Lori with other students who have mastered the same skills for some face-to-face, real-life, exercises.

Customer-focused education: exploration of the self

Angela is now back in her silent cubicle writing a letter. Some time ago, Angela chose to find her identical friend through a module that offered hundreds of qualitative questions for participants all over the world to answer. The questions are designed to explore opinions, judgments, expectations, likes, dislikes, learning, experiences, perceptions, behaviors, and every possible emotion. The goal is to help the individual discover a great deal about himself or herself and at the same time build a unique profile.

The computer has reported that a close match to Angela's profile is a girl named Sally—about Angela's age—from a city half-way across the country. Sally wrote to Angela, via computer mail, and Angela is writing Sally a letter in return.

As Angela is writing the letter, she is only aware of her interest in her pen pal and her curiosity to discover how alike they are. Angela doesn't feel self-conscious about sharing her innermost feelings with the computer, because she knows the computer isn't human, or a real person, and she trusts it.

Even personal tasks, such as writing letters to a friend, become opportunities for instruction and learning.

Customer-focused education: surveying opportunities

Unaware of the drama playing out in the cubicle next to her, Felicia is busy speaking in German to a computer-simulated person speaking in Italian. The computer interrupts the dialogue with a request that Felicia attend a session of advanced Spanish speakers and act as the group's facilitator. The computer prints out a series of exercises and a facilitation plan, allowing Felicia to go off to the assigned group room and conduct the group session.

Meetings can be called and held at the convenience of the students participating. None of the individual or group learning have to wait for school periods to begin or end.

Customer-focused education: the group rooms

Leaving the silent cubicles, we move on to a series of larger rooms available for meetings of groups. Groups are used for a variety of purposes in the new paradigm schools. Here is a brief look at some of the groups.

An interest group

In this room is an interest group meeting for the purpose of discussing the career that they are all "trying out." Each person in this group is studying what it would be like to be an architect. It doesn't matter that the group is made up of students of different ages, or different levels of prior education. The participants expect to find students of different ages. All share the common interest of learning about becoming architects.

A synthesis group

The next group room contains a synthesis group. These students are all trying out what it would be like to be attorneys, and they have all advanced past the recall and understanding modules and are deep into application of their skills.

Synthesis groups give students the opportunity to add to the building blocks they have mastered, and combine two or more concepts from the building blocks to form newly created conclusions. Synthesis groups are all guided by teachers who have mastered the advanced instruction in the career, interest, or life skill being studied.

A performance group

In the next room, we can observe a play being performed for a small audience. The play is put on by people trying out what it would be like to be an actor. The play was written by an individual who has mastered what it would be like to be a playwright. The audience is made up of other students who are also learning what it is like to be actors, who will observe the play as part of their education. The rest of the audience is made up of people who have chosen to watch plays as one of their ways of taking a break from the intensity of their own instruction.

A celebration group

In the next room we find a group of young people gathering to celebrate the achievement of learning goals. Each of these people, in turn, is asked to tell what they have learned, describe something valuable that they discovered in the learning, and tell the group what they intend to learn next.

A language group

In the next group room we find Felicia leading a group of students in Spanish. She is facilitating the group as it follows the instructions for exercises that each individual has been given by the computer.

The laboratories

The laboratories in new paradigm schools are similar to the silent cubicles, but different in terms of equipment. The laboratories are equipped with extraordinarily powerful computers. The powerful computers are needed because the laboratories are conducted via "virtual reality."

Virtual reality is a world that is only possible with high-powered computers and special programming. The idea of virtual reality is that the computer simulates reality in such a way that the student can interact with it, and the virtual reality reacts in the way that *real* reality would. Some examples are be useful:

Shannon looks at atoms with a virtual-reality electron microscope using the video display to simulate the view of real objects.

Shannon can adjust the viewfinder to show the object, or zoom in on any level she chooses, down to and beyond the atom. A "real" electron microscope is extremely expensive, and would not be available to a student in an ordinary school.

Sandy is dissecting a "live" frog. In old paradigm biology classes, students could only work with dead animals. Public sentiment, as well as natural human squeamishness, argued against dissecting animals while they were alive.

Using "virtual reality," however, we can observe Sandy opening up a "virtually live" frog, which exists only in the creative imagination of the computer. By donning a pair of glasses that beam video pictures into her eyes, Sandy truly feels as though she is in a laboratory. When Sandy cuts it, it bleeds. When she opens it up, she can observe all of the functions operating normally. When she finishes her dissection, she can choose to back out of the procedure and find the "virtually real" frog untouched by her exploration.

Mr. Gillig is changing a tire on his car

In the next cubicle, Mr. Gillig has come in to learn how to change the tire on his car. Mr. Gillig feels helpless around mechanical things and has allowed them to terrify him for much of his life.

Mr. Gillig has now discovered virtual reality, and its power to simulate the most complex, or most simple of realities. With the computer screen, an automobile maintenance program, and computer "gloves," he can simulate each step in the process of changing a tire. He could also open up the engine and watch it while it works, if he were to choose. At this stage, however, he is content to just learn the basics that will make him feel safer while driving.

Dorothy plays her viola with the Israel Philharmonic Orchestra conducted by Zubin Mehta

Dorothy practices each day with the ordinary computer simulation at her own learning cubicle. She feels ready now to discover what it would be like to play with a world-class orchestra.

Using virtual reality in the lab, the computer recreates an orchestral performance of Mozart's "Sinfonia concertante" with Itzhak Perlman and Pinchas Zukerman playing the solo parts. Through the magic of virtual reality, she can substitute for Pinchas Zuckerman and play with Perlman and the orchestra.

Combining the magic of computer-driven glasses, and the magic of computer-driven digital television, she can watch her fellow musicians, and hear the music as she would hear it if she were indeed playing with the Israel Philharmonic.

Henry is landing a 747 at Heathrow Airport in the fog

Henry has moved from the relative comfort of small screen at his silent cubicle, to the power of virtual reality to simulate landing a Boeing 747 at London's Heathrow Airport.

We could stay and watch, but we could only watch on the computer monitor, and we wouldn't be experiencing the same "virtual reality" that Henry is experiencing through his computer-driven video glasses.

The cafeteria

The cafeteria is similar to old paradigm cafeterias, with a few notable exceptions. As the educational system is debureaucratized, it becomes clear that schools can serve a broader role in society than simply providing teaching. The schools can be used all day as part of the food delivery system for the elderly and the needy. Anyone is welcome. Parents can come sometimes to have meals with their children. Grandparents can come sometimes to visit and eat with their grandchildren. School cafeterias in the new paradigm are managed using the strategies and techniques used in the private sector.

In private-sector restaurants, the management has to predict daily how many customers may appear, and yet, somehow, they almost always have enough food to handle the crowd.

The day-care center

The day-care center is where pre-schoolers and other children stay after school until there is an adult at home. Buses run throughout the day on planned schedules, bringing adult students and children to and from school. In situations where parents find it difficult to deliver or pick up their children from school or day care, they are transported by school buses.

School buses are also integrated into the public transportation system of the community and, where possible and practical, school buses serve the public as well as students.

Because every new paradigm school has access to the same quality and level of instruction, equality of education has been realized without the necessity of "busing" children far from their homes. The money that school systems have saved by eliminating extensive busing has been used to hire more teachers.

The gymnasium

Young people show up for sports or exercise better prepared than they did in the old paradigm because they have learned more skills through simulation and life skills instruction. There has been little significant change, however, in sports or games or exercises that develop the student physically.

The library—the "brain" center

There are still books in the library, but they're used much less. All textual resources are available through the computer and pages can be printed out at will, so there is less need for books. The major use of the library in the new paradigm is to house the computer equipment and data used locally at the school.

The principles underlying the new paradigm

With this vision of public education (circa 2013) in mind, it is helpful to examine the underlying principles of the new public education paradigm.

In the old paradigm, it can be effectively argued that the mission of the school is to serve "the public." The problem with serving "the public" is that it is too amorphous. The "public" is everyone. So, the schools end up serving the superintendent, or the school board, or the legislature, or worse yet, all of the above. The mission is up-focused rather than focused on the customer—the student.

The old paradigm educational system is organized based on the bureaucratic organizing model:

1. Hierarchical agency—decisions are made at the top of the agency (e.g., the state, the school board, the superintendent), rather than at a level closer to the student.

2. Control via rules—the judgment of the teacher may be superseded by rules made by people far away from the place where students learn.

3. An up-focused mission—serves those that charter or fund it.

4. Purposely impersonal—equal treatment for everyone, regardless of human differences or individual need.

5. Organized by specialty or function—each discipline is taught separately (math, science, language, history, etc.).

The new paradigm is based on the idea that schools need to have specific customers, and need to serve these customers effectively. The mission-driven model facilitates customer-focused learning:

1. Empowered, multi-disciplinary teams make the decisions, at the closest possible level to the student. (This replaces the hierarchical structure.)

2. Guidelines are used, where possible, to replace rules. Teachers, mentors, and other learning support people are empowered to put aside the guidelines, and use their judgment, when the guidelines interfere with mission achievement—learning.

3. The mission in a mission-driven school is customer focused, rather than up-focused, as stated above.

4. Instead of being purposely impersonal, the school and all of its people are encouraged to consider the human and individual needs of each of their students, and their co-workers. Equal satisfaction can only be achieved through unequal treatment.

5. Instead of organizing by specialty or function, the mission-driven agency organizes people into multi-disciplinary teams, and it organizes information into multi-disciplinary "contexts."

From teaching to learning

The old paradigm educational system concentrates on teaching. The new paradigm focuses on learning. Traditional forms of teaching may or may not be the best way to achieve that goal.

The old paradigm educational system places the control, and thus the responsibility for teaching on the teacher. The new paradigm places the control (and responsibility) of learning on the student. Teaching is measured as good or bad based on its usefulness to the student in helping that student learn.

It has been widely known by educators of every discipline that the optimal form of learning is through individualized instruction. In the current educational system, individualized instruction is impossible financially, because it would require one teacher for each student.

The only practical way for public education to offer individualized instruction is through the use of technology. In the past, educators experimented with CAI (computer aided instruction) and "teaching machines" with mixed results.

These "teaching machines" simulated traditional "teaching." The machines did not focus on motivating or stimulating the student, or keeping the student's interest. They often did not result in learning. While there were some successes, many students found the machines boring. Additionally, many educators and administrators found the idea of teaching machines threatening. Some saw their jobs at stake. Even those who welcomed the technology found it difficult to integrate individualized instruction into their rigidly regimented classrooms and schools.

Finally, finding money to fund technological advances in the classroom was a problem. To buy new equipment, schools often would have had to stretch their existing budgets, which meant that each department would fight hard to keep *their* portion of the budget from being reduced.

The vision for the new paradigm is based on several assumptions that seem possible and reasonable. To begin with, no new technological breakthroughs are required to realize the vision presented above. The technology exists right now.

With a national set of "open" standards, software producers could produce programming that wouldn't be made obsolete by changes in hardware, operating systems, or student monitoring programs. Software programs would thus be subject to risk only from competing software that is more appealing or elegant rather from obsolescence.

If a global library of programs were accessible by every school, then producers of programs wouldn't have to sell the program to each individual school system. This would reduce the cost of selling, and reduce the return needed by the program producers in order to invest. A central library would also assure that even the poorest school in the poorest land would have access to the most powerful learning, as long as their school had the necessary delivery equipment.

In this vision, I assumed an international market, in which the computer manufacturers accept the risk for technological obsolescence and for capital investment. I think that the agreed-upon set of "open" standards will protect the investment of the computer manufacturers. I think the manufacturers will choose modular and upgradable design strategies for producing school hardware to minimize the costs of obsolescence.

Finally, I have assumed that dissatisfaction with the existing educational system is so widespread the educators and citizens alike will be open to allowing private-sector firms to join in alliance with educators to produce a joint public/private solution.

Learning in context

Those who have studied "natural" learning have found that people are motivated to learn by a variety of sources, including curiosity, survival, economic or social gain, the need for stimulation, etc. "Natural" learning is learner driven.

When learning occurs "naturally," it virtually always occurs within a "context." For example, people who are unable to read may decide to learn in order to achieve some practical objective, such as qualifying for a job, finding their way through town, etc.

If we are to attract students to learning, we must offer them instruction that "fits" naturally into the context of what they want to know. Few students, for instance, want to learn geometry as a subject on its own. Yet many will learn geometry eagerly if it will help them navigate an airplane.

The desire to learn partly depends on the "flow" produced by the learning—which attracts students by itself—and by the potential gain the student sees from achieving the learning. Students will be most strongly motivated to learn if the process will offer them some benefit they seek.

Students seek a variety of different benefits, and each student is different. Additionally, each student changes and has changing needs over the course of time.

To remain a constantly stimulating, exciting, and motivating learning environment, the learning modules must aim for a wide range of possible student benefits. Some modules might offer economic gain by equipping the student for well-paid work. Other modules might offer the opportunity to help others by equipping the student to become part of the helping professions. Some modules might offer increased social acceptance by equipping the student to make friends easily or work well with others. Some modules might offer help in finding a "significant other" by equipping the student with social and bonding skills.

The idea is to offer a wide variety of contexts that meet a wide variety of perceived needs in students, all offering continuous improvement in the basic skills of reading, writing, experimenting, and calculating, along with a survey of the core studies that will provide a structure for understanding human, group, organizational, national, and international events.

The Heuristic model

The new paradigm assumes that computer programs can be produced that will use heuristic learning strategies to gradually learn how to guide a given student. These programs could be made to serve the student by monitoring the student's activities, attention, and learning rates. The monitoring programs would adjust the rate of instruction to keep the individual student in a balance of "flow."

The student would be provided with the optimal balance of challenge and capabilities. The learning rate would be sufficient to keep the student from being bored, and yet not so rapid that the student becomes frustrated. The educational system of the future would tailor this learning rate to each person, adapting to the daily changes of the individual and to the student's differing abilities in any discipline, from math to reading.

Lifetime learning

The new paradigm is built on the idea of "lifetime learning." Rather than grouping the students into groups by age or learning capacity or speed of learning, the new system groups them by common interest, learning achieved, or roles required.

These groups are not static or "fixed," but change as the students change. They form, work, achieve, and then break up. As learning progresses, and individual student's needs change, the groups change as well. These dynamic groups ensure that each participant is equipped to contribute to the group and that each participant is highly valued.

Students will stay in school as long as they are challenged, motivated, and stimulated by learning, and as long as the learning is leading them to some desired outcome. When the student sees the benefits of leaving school outweigh the benefits of staying in school, that student is ready to enter the work world, service world, government, or scholarship.

If, over time, the student's needs and desires change, or the chosen career changes, the student can return to school.

The old paradigm schools "reject" as many as one of every three students that enter. These dropouts, who often fail to learn what they need to know to contribute to society and earn their own way, represent an enormous drain on our society. With the new paradigm schools, we stand a chance at salvaging many of these people that the old educational system has failed.

Channel the brainpower and entrepreneurship of America's most creative and talented

The United States is shifting away from its enormous investment in defense at the same time that the critical national need for education reform is being recognized.

The new paradigm offers a solution to the problem of what to do with the capital, talent, and brainpower that have been assembled for the defense establishment. It makes sense as a matter of national educational policy to stimulate the redirection of those talents to the creation of the hardware and software systems that can produce individualized learning.

Those concerned with the ability of the U.S. to compete globally should note that this country already leads the world in the usage of computers and in the design and usage of software. If the U.S. decides to capitalize on those strengths, it is possible that the U.S. could take a global leadership role in providing "space age" educational opportunities to students throughout the world.

The new paradigm school is based on the notion that government does a better job of "steering" than "rowing." It can be argued that the state of the existing education system is the result of asking a government built on bureaucracy to operate an educational system, which requires constant growth and change.

By thoughtful division of roles we can get the best from all parties to the equation. New paradigm education will require the capital investment needed to equip every child, in every school, with access to a computer. It will require enormous investment in creative software that produces learning on an individualized basis. These investments and the re-direction of the talents necessary to produce the hardware and software needed are only available from private-sector firms that would invest with hopes of profits from their success.

Government's role in the new paradigm would be to set the standards that would make the marketplace work. Government's role would be to bring together, and perhaps assure the success of collaborative alliances between educators and the private sector. Finally, government would set standards against which the continuous improvement of learning achieved by students could be measured.

Chapter Thirteen

What if?

What might change in government if it could put aside the bureaucratic organizing model?

Continuing the same type of exercise as in the last chapter, suppose, for a moment, that agencies were not focused so narrowly on their tiny spectrum of social problems. Suppose it were possible to focus on outcomes, not processes, and that individual agencies were required to "nest" their missions within a larger state-wide, province-wide, or nation-wide mission.

Some whimsical examples:

Suppose the U.S. Department of Justice, which is concerned with law enforcement and maintaining the prison system, got together with the State Department, which is responsible for considering the needs of neighboring nations. Sprinkle in some creativity and the U.S. Congress might consider legislation to allow other countries to bid on housing our "career" criminals (those willing to forfeit their rights to constitutional protection by committing three or more felonies.)

Jailing our career criminals in Mexico, San Salvador, or Panama would benefit those countries by infusing capital for construction of jails, and jobs for citizens from those countries as jailers, cooks, wardens, etc. At the same time, politicians would not have to struggle with voters who don't want more prisons in their neighborhoods. By accepting the lowest bidders, we could house our criminals much more cheaply than we do currently.

Suppose the people responsible for welfare, who are concerned with providing for the poor and homeless, got together with the State Department. We might achieve what many have so long yearned for—the ability to make poor people affluent. At some point in the welfare cycle, if an individual gives up hope or stops trying to be self-sufficient, then that person could be put on a pension in a foreign country, at much less than it costs to keep that person on welfare in the United States. In Bolivia, Peru, or Haiti, or other nations, an amount that would keep them in poverty in the United States would allow them to live very well.

This would stimulate the economy of those nations and create service jobs. From some viewpoints, one could say that "everybody wins." The proverbial "welfare mother" that so infuriates conservatives could, at a lower cost than present welfare costs, have a relatively luxurious home in another nearby nation.

These notions are not presented as serious proposals. They are of-
fered as examples of what "synergy" becomes possible when you step
out of the bureaucratic box of looking only at one problem at a time.

Idea #1

One strategy would be to use the bureaucratic process itself to reduce the negative effects of bureaucracy on the citizenry. For example, we could ask legislators to pass regulations linking agency
funding with citizen-satisfaction ratings. This strategy would help
governmental agencies balance their up-focus with a customer focus.

The people in those agencies would welcome our support and
appreciate our help in giving them a clear charter to satisfy customers. In addition, the agencies would then have a clear mandate
to collect customer feedback, which they could use to drive higher
and higher satisfaction scores.

We could ask legislators to pass regulations requiring that budget
cuts first affect those above the line, and people below the line last.
This would keep agencies from becoming "top-heavy, bottom-lean."
Better yet, it might totally erase the line.

Idea #2

Let's give the governmental bureaucracies more competition from
nonprofit agencies and private enterprise. This competition will
help them become less in-focused and more customer focused. It's
harder to fall back into bureaucratic ways when competitive forces
are at work. While we are waiting for the educational system of the
future, let's give private enterprise a chance at the kids that public
education has given up on. If the private sector produces good results, let's install their products in our public schools. If we are truly
going to achieve our ambitions for our children, we have to help our
long-suffering, under-appreciated teachers and administrators
overcome the immobilizing effects of bureaucracy.

Let's privatize more of the functions now handled by agencies of
government. Whenever possible, let government oversee rather
than actually doing the work.

As we privatize, let's make sure that we relax the grip that bureaucracy has on the privatized agencies. For example, the United

States has had both public and private schools for a long time. If you ask private schools, however, they'll tell you that they have to conform to many, if not all, of the same rules and suffocating structure that immobilize public education. To be accredited and to have grades and transcripts accepted by other institutions, private schools are forced to accommodate their curricula and instructional processes to suit the bureaucracy's norms of public education.

Some observers argue that privatization doesn't always work to produce market sensitivity and effectiveness in agencies that once were run by government. I suggest that we look carefully at each case of failed privatization to see if the bureaucratic controls were lifted, and if the agency was allowed to shift from a bureaucratic agency to a mission-driven agency.

Private ownership, by itself, only adds additional pressure for profitability to a formerly governmental agency, which can be just another way of producing an up-focused or in-focused mission. To achieve its full potential, privatized agencies must be given some flexibility or they'll succumb to the same bureaucratic immobilization that afflicts many governmental agencies.

Idea #3

Let's stop turning our problems over to government if it is going to try to solve them through bureaucratic processes. Bureaucracies are limited to a few processes and are process driven rather than results driven.

For example, few people think that the U.S. Veterans Administration runs better hospitals or gives veterans better care than they could receive from the "normal" doctors and hospitals. It's highly probable that we could give the veterans better care, with less bureaucratic red tape, and for less money than they currently get from the Veterans Administration.

Idea #4:

We could go all the way and help government agencies adopt a new model to replace the bureaucratic model. I suggest we not define the "process," but rather define the outcomes we want. We could evaluate our agencies using some sort of modified "Malcolm Baldrige Award" criteria, and allocate resources based on success in meeting the criteria.

We could ask our lawmakers to pass legislation creating "replacement" agencies, organized on the non-bureaucratic model. The lawmakers could then transfer the burdens away from our most immobilized bureaucracies to the replacement agencies.

We would then find out if new agencies, organized in a different way, can't do a better job for the citizenry. Remember, it isn't the people in government, it's the organizing model. *I've seen people hired into my company, who have worked in bureaucratic agencies for years, put bureaucratic behaviors aside and become mission-driven almost overnight.*

A summary of conclusions

The bureaucratic organizing model is the most common organizing model for public-sector organizations throughout the world. The bureaucratic model does not produce organizations that are extraordinary at satisfying customers or achieving "quality" in their products.

Bureaucracy seems to produce the highest levels of personal satisfaction for those at the top of an agency. Those people at the bottom, and *not* coincidently, closest to the customers, are far less personally satisfied with the bureaucracy.

Agencies tend to become bureaucratic when permitted, but nothing suggests that they cannot become responsive, customer-focused, and truly public-service oriented, if encouraged.

Each government agency is given some form of monopoly. Each agency is organized as a bureaucracy. Government agencies come in dead last when consumers are asked to evaluate organizations in terms of "productivity," "quality," or "service."

Monopoly is the major ally of bureaucracy. Bureaucratic agencies survive only because they are granted some level of monopoly and because no other agency is chartered to do what they do. Unmodified bureaucratic organizations need not earn customer satisfaction to survive; they only require appropriations.

The devastating results are evident everywhere. The citizens get poor results for their taxes, and they blame it on politicians or people in government, yet the people in government are victims of a poor organizing model. Politicians do their best to bring about meaningful change, and their efforts are defeated by government workers trapped in a system immobilized by bureaucracy.

It is time to recognize the real villain, the bureaucratic organizing model. Citizens, politicians, appointees, and government workers are all victimized by bureaucracy.

Assertions and observations

- There is no legitimate reason for any public-sector organization that aspires to deliver products or customer-satisfying service to continue using the bureaucratic organizational form.

- Many agencies are installing "quality" programs as part of their search for excellence as well as a cure for the symptoms of bureaucracy. Most are using some form of steering committees, task forces, or action teams to implement "quality" in their organizations. The underlying bureaucracy will defeat these efforts unless these special committees are organized in a "mission-driven" form (a non-bureaucratic form described in this book). We have never seen a bureaucratically organized committee or task force cure a bureaucratic agency of poor quality or service.

- The employees of bureaucratic agencies suffer the most. The more bureaucratic the agency is, the more stress, anxiety, and anger the employees have.

- The health and success of our government in the future may depend more on organizational structure than on the amount of funding it receives or the nature of the problems it encounters.

Exciting possibilities

- We have alternatives to entrusting our most difficult national issues to bureaucratic governmental agencies. We can make it possible for some government agencies to become mission driven, (a non-bureaucratic organizing form described herein). We can allow more competition from the private sector.

- I believe that a combination of private enterprise and purposeful debureaucratization will make it possible to overcome the bureaucratic paralysis that immobilizes public education in the United States. The vision offered in this book for a "customer-focused" education system is so powerful and so compelling that I predict the bureaucratic educational system will adopt it and bring it to life, or else the citizenry will "privatize" education, and replace the existing educational system and its bureaucracy.

This book outlines a set of steps for debureaucratizing by changing basic organizing principles:

a. Make an assessment of the present state of the agency to learn how much permission to change and commitment to change is available from funding entities, the Administration, and top agency officials.

b. Depending on the climate for change and resources committed for change, choose the optimal goal state: a modest goal, a moderate goal, or an ambitious goal.

c. The goal state will suggest the strategy for changing the agency. The strategy will range from a minimum effort based mostly on training, to a maximum effort based on reorganization and a new way of managing called "continuous improvement."

d. Continuous improvement is an entirely new way of operating in which the people closest to the customer, working in teams, are empowered to continuously improve the agency's quality, service, or both. Continuous improvement requires three things:

   1. A "shadow" organization chartered to make the changes necessary in the existing agency to achieve the desired goal state.

   2. New forms of qualitative customer feedback from internal and external customers to be used to drive changes in quality, service, or both.

   3. Training for employees enabling them to work in teams, to accept the offered empowerment, to identify and prioritize root causes of problems, and to find solutions they will use to continually improve quality, service, or both.

Managers in the existing agency will need to learn and use new ways of managing. They will need to learn what they have been doing that adds to the bureaucracy in the agency. They will need to learn new ways of doing their jobs that will diminish the amount of bureaucracy. Most importantly, they will need to provide empowerment for those who work for them, and protection and coaching to those who accept and act upon the offered empowerment.

Non-managers will play a vital new role in the debureaucratized agency. The employee/management war, if it exists in your agency, must end. Everyone in the agency will need to act as part of one unified team, driven by a common mission, and aligned by a common vision of the new agency. People who today are not formally managing will be grouped into teams in which the brainpower, skills, talents, and experience of the individuals will be harnessed to continually improve the agency's quality, service, or both.

Afterword

If you're attempting to debureaucratize to a significant degree, you will have to move beyond the unit level. If this book contains ideas that your boss might like to see, by all means, pass it up the line. If enough copies of this book are passed up the line, great things can happen, especially when the Secretary or Head of your agency finds five or six copies on his/her desk.

Select Bibliography

Books

Johnston, Kenneth B. *Busting Bureaucracy.* Homewood, IL: Business One Irwin, 1992.

Yoho, Dave, and Jeff Davidson. *How To Have A Good Year Every Year.* New York: Berkley Books, 1991.

Articles

"News In Brief." *Federal Quality News,* vol. 1, no. 2 (March 1992).

"Results." *Federal Quality News,* vol. 1, no. 3 (July 1992).

Lang, Alexandra. "Commitment to Service Quality Revitalized in Georgia." *in-touch Magazine.* Tampa, FL: Kaset International (Winter 1989).

Levin, Blair. "Realism Begs for Government 'Improvement.'" *Triangle Business News* (August 31, 1992).

Wood, Patricia. "How Quality is Being Achieved." *National Productivity Review* (Spring 1992): 257-264.

Zemke, Ron. "Putting the Service Back Into Public Service." *Training* (November 1989).

Reports

Auditor General of Canada. "Well-Performing Organizations." *Extract from the Report of the Auditor General of Canada to the House of Commons.* Ontario: 1988.

"Quality Improvement Prototype Award." *Five Case Studies.* Washington, D.C.: Federal Quality Institute, 1992.